A Williamson *Little Hands*® Book

Sing! Play! Create!

☺ Hands-On Learning for 3- to 7-year-olds ☺

Lisa Boston

Illustrated by Sarah Cole

**WILLIAMSON BOOKS
NASHVILLE, TN**

Library of Congress Cataloging-in-Publication Data
Boston, Lisa.
  Sing! play! create! : hands-on learning for 3- to 7-year-olds / Lisa Boston ; illustrations by Sarah Cole.
     p. cm. — (A Williamson Little Hands book)
  Includes index.
  ISBN 0-8249-6780-1 (softcover : alk. paper) — ISBN 0-8249-6781-X (casebound : alk. paper)
  1. Early childhood education—Activity programs. 2. Creative activities and seat work. I. Cole, Sarah, ill. II. Title. III. Series.

LB1139.35.A37B67 2006
372.21—dc22

2005030453

Little Hands® series editor: **Susan Williamson**
Project editor: **Emily Stetson**
Interior design: **Sydney Wright**
Illustrations: **Sarah Cole**
Cover design and cover illustrations: **Michael Kline**

Published by Williamson Books
An imprint of Ideals Publications
535 Metroplex Drive, Suite 250
Nashville, Tennessee 37211
800-586-2572

Printed and bound in China
10 9 8 7 6 5 4 3 2 1

Dedication

To my children, Janice and Shaun, and to my husband, Aric. I love you!

Acknowledgments

I'd like to thank my parents, Frank & Carol Hunter, for their love and support and for being actively involved parents; Gymboree, for being there for me as a new parent and for teaching me the joy and importance of music and play; Aric, Janice, and Shaun, for their moral and endless technical support; everyone at CSGT, for their willingness to help out, especially Penny Liberman and Laura Beals, my quality control team; Alix Liberman, for her enthusiasm; Williamson Publishing, for making this book a reality; and all the parents and children who have shared a part of their lives with me at Gymboree and World Discoveries.

Songs: The following lyrics were written by the author: *Acacia Tree, The* (pg. 73), *All Around the Farmyard* (pg. 95), *Billy Goat, Billy Goat* (pg. 114), *Brown Bear, Brown Bear* (pg. 82), *Butterfly, Butterfly Turn Around* (pg. 56), *Butterfly Chant* (pg. 54), *Buzzing Little Bees* (pg. 44), *Chomp, Chomp Went the Little Green Alligator* (pg. 33), *Clippity-Clop* (pg. 106), *Creepy, Crawly Caterpillar* (pg. 51), *Dragonfly* (pg. 18), *Elephants' Twist, The* (pg. 66), *Giraffe and the Tall, Tall Tree, The* (pg. 74), *Go In & Out the Barn Door* (pg. 92), *Hungry, Hungry Hippo* (pg. 75), *Hungry Little Alligator* (pg. 35), *I'm A Little Turtle* (pg. 25), *I'm Going Fishing* (pg. 24), *I'm Picking Flowers* (pg. 43), *Kangaroo Hop* (pg. 85), *Lion Pokey* (pg. 71), *Mother Hen* (pg. 100), *My Little House Up on a Hill* (pg. 57), *One Little Lion at the Zoo* (pg. 69), *Piggilty, Piggilty, Pop* (pg. 121), *Pretty Peacock* (pg. 90), *Quack, Quack Went the Little Yellow Duck* (pg. 29), *Ribbet, Ribbet* (pg. 14), *Seeds to Flowers* (pg. 41), *Slither, Slide & Hiss* (pg. 62), *Ten Little Cows in the Barn* (pg. 107), *This is the Way We Plant Our Garden* (pg. 40), *Three Little Turkeys Went Out to Play* (pg. 118), *Two Little Snails* (pg. 61)

The following lyrics are Traditional: *Five Little Monkeys* (pg. 79), *Hokey Pokey, The* (pg. 71), *I'm A Little Teapot,* (pg. 25), Itsy Bitsy Spider *(Ladybug), The* (pg. 48), *Mary Had a Little Lamb* (pg. 111), *Mulberry Bush, The* (pg. 40), *Row, Row, Row Your Boat* (pg. 10).

All other lyrics, including *Ten Little Fishies in the Pond,* aka *Fishies in the Ocean* (pg. 21), are unknown. The author would be grateful to anyone who can identify the original sources.

Contents

Sing, Play, Create ... NOW!

This book is for teachers, parents, caregivers, librarians, and — most of all — children everywhere. Use it to extend a lesson plan, enrich story time, provide focus and fun for playgroup get-togethers, encourage everyday creativity, spark up a rainy day, enhance a birthday party theme, and create lasting memories. The important thing is to begin!

Through my years of teaching and working with large and small groups of children and through the time spent with my own two children, I've discovered that the following tips encourage positive experiences.

Keep It Simple!

All the activities in this book use items that are readily available. Before starting a craft or game, read through the activity and set out the materials that you will be using. Don't hesitate to substitute materials listed in an activity for materials that you have on hand. Consider creating a basic craft supply box and game box (page 8) so that you'll be prepared for any playtime or crafting opportunity.

Feel free to vary the materials for the craft projects and games. An activity might suggest using paint, but it could also be created with collage, crayons, or markers. Each technique encourages and enhances fine motor skills, eye-hand coordination, and sensory awareness. So be creative and try making the same project using a variety of methods.

Be Spontaneous and Have Fun!

Follow the needs and interests of the child. A young child might start out cutting paper to create a collage, for example, and decide to spend the rest of the day cutting paper into small pieces! Appreciate that he is developing his fine motor skills and building a foundation for later learning. Put the pieces of cut paper in a baggy and save them for another time. Similarly, let the child lead and do the creating. Resist the temptation to take over a project, and remember that there is no "right way" to do it. The process, not the final product, is key.

A child's art reflects her developmental stage. If a project seems too difficult, modify the instructions to make it easier, or try the same project again in a few weeks or months.

Conversely, use easy projects as a springboard for creating additional challenges. Two-year-olds will probably need you to do most of the preparation (cutting, stapling, tying, and so on) and will be fascinated exploring the mediums (painting, gluing, coloring). Three- and four-year-olds usually want to do it all by themselves, but actually they will still need assistance. Older children tend to be more self-sufficient and will spend more time working on details, but they will still request assistance from time to time.

Keep It Safe!

- Protect work surfaces with a plastic tablecloth or newspaper. Have paper towels handy for spills and messy fingers.

- Use washable, non-toxic materials. Protect clothing by wearing an apron or an old shirt.

- Evaluate each child's ability to use scissors, staplers, and hole punches safely.

- Be aware of children who tend to put objects in their mouth and adjust materials appropriately.

- Set up all games in a safe environment.

- Supervise young children at all times and be especially attentive while creating crafts and playing games.

Glue. Young artists have an easier time applying glue that is already in a small dish. If covering large areas, use a chunky paintbrush to paint glue onto the project and then add the collage materials. For smaller projects, use a fine paintbrush to apply the glue directly to the collage item. When introducing children to using a glue bottle, limit the flow of glue by adjusting the opening in the lid. Supervise closely, as a child's natural tendency will be to practice this new skill by emptying the entire bottle!

FRINGE

BEAK

HEAD

BODY

step 1

step 3

Scissors. Young children should always use child-safety scissors. Invest in a quality pair of scissors that can be used by left- or right-handed children. If you have a hard time using the scissors, the child will find it almost impossible!

Young children usually do not have the fine motor skills necessary to use scissors with one hand. Initially, the child should hold the scissors with both hands, one on the top and the other on the bottom. Assist the child by holding the paper taut as he cuts.

   Collage materials. The art of collage involves using glue, scissors, and collage materials. Collage artwork is as unique as the items used to create the collage. Materials are suggested in each of the collage projects, but do not be limited by those suggestions. For example, I suggest covering the rooster puppet (page 98) with feathers. If you don't have feathers or you would prefer using other materials, improvise with anything from scraps of felt or wallpaper to twigs collected outdoors.

Take Time

Children grow up fast! Take the time to enjoy, appreciate, and share each stage of this wonderful time in a child's life. My hope is that you will create memories through the activities you find here. Children may not remember the crafts, the games, or all the words to the songs when they are grown, but surely they will remember the warm feeling of spending time together. Enjoy!

ABOUT THIS BOOK

Each project is a complete unit with a song, craft, and game, along with a drawing segment for some. Pick and choose the activities that you want to do in any order that you want to do them. One day you may feel like creating a quick craft, and another day you may be looking for activities to fill up an entire afternoon. You may want to complete the projects in thematic units or by the project that most interests the child.

 Let's Sing

In this section you will find lyrics along with movements for interacting with the words. I suggest a tune for singing the lyrics. If you don't know the tune, make up your own melody or sing it to the tune of another song that you do know. All of the lyrics can also be done as chants.

Children learn through repetition, so when introducing new songs or chants, repeat them several times. Sing songs from previous projects as well. I like to sing two to three songs with each craft. For an interactive story time, alternate reading books with singing songs.

Let's Create

The goal of creating crafts with children is to explore a variety of art mediums, to expand imaginations, to enhance fine motor skills, and to have fun. The goal is not to make an exact replica of a rooster, duck, or

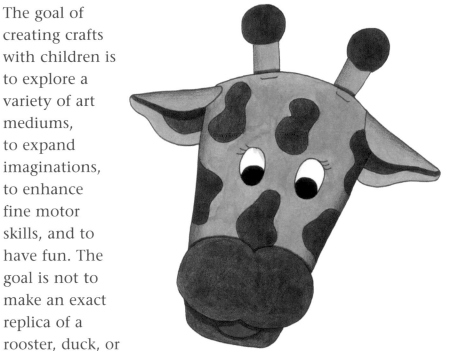

giraffe. Be happy with a project that the child is proud of, and let the child explain her artwork. Enjoy the child's delight in her accomplishment and in sharing it with you.

Let's Play

Games promote physical activity as well as providing opportunities for social interaction and cooperation. Repetition is important for children to become comfortable with the game format and reap the maximum benefits. Games are presented in a non-competitive format where everyone is encouraged to cheer each other on. The games can easily be adapted to small or large groups.

Let's Draw

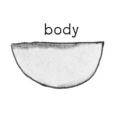

Many two-year-olds can draw a squiggle on a piece of paper and then imagine that it is the bird that they had pictured in their mind. They think nothing of picking up a pencil or crayon and drawing with amazing confidence. Encourage and treasure this time, for even as they are refining their fine motor skills, all too soon most children lose this innocence and succumb to feelings of artistic inadequacy because things don't "look right." In the LET'S DRAW sections, children are encouraged to see the simple shapes in an object. Again, the goal is not to create a perfect rooster, duck, or giraffe. The goal is to provide the child with a satisfying drawing experience.

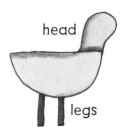

body

head

legs

eye and beak

wing

feet

Craft Box

A craft box consists of basic "purchased" supplies (glue, stapler, construction paper, paper plates), along with plenty of household collectibles such as paper-towel tubes and egg cartons. These are some of the things I use frequently:

Child-safety scissors
Collage materials (sequins, pom-poms, etc.)
Construction paper
Contact paper (clear)
Cotton balls
Craft or Popsicle sticks
Craft feathers
Crayons
Egg cartons
Glue or glue stick
Hole punch
Jar lids
Markers
Nature finds (shells, pebbles, bark)
Paintbrushes (assorted sizes)
Paints (dot paints, poster/tempera paints, watercolors)

Paper bags (lunch & grocery size)
Paper cups
Paper-towel & toilet-paper tubes
Pencils
Pipe cleaners
Plastic drinking straws
Poster board, card stock
Odd socks
Old magazines
Sponges
Stapler
Stickers
Tape
Tissue paper
Wiggly eyes
Yarn
Yogurt containers with lids
Zipper-style plastic bags

Game Box

Hours of fun can be had with just a few basic items and a touch of imagination! These are some of the items that I recommend:

Balls, Baskets, Beanbags, Cardboard boxes, Carpet squares, Cones, Hula hoops, Kitchen timer, Paper grocery bags, Scarves, Sheets or blankets, Socks, Soft drink bottles, Stuffed animals

At the Pond

At the pond on a lazy day,
Fishing and boating, you're invited to stay.

Waddle like a duck, hop with the frogs,
Create a turtle, sunning on a log.

Use binoculars to take in the sights,
Spy a fish, or a dragonfly in flight.

At the pond the adventure will begin,
So turn on your imagination, and join right in!

Pond Play

A pond is the home of many animals and plants. Fish swim in the water, insects skim and buzz across the water's surface, and frogs and turtles sun on the rocks and hide in the mud at the water's edge. What will you see in your imaginary pond? Make some binoculars, take a look, and create your own pretend pond view!

 Let's Sing

Row, Row, Row Your Boat
(Traditional tune, or chant)

Row, row, row your boat,
Gently down the stream.

Merrily, merrily, merrily, merrily,
Life is but a dream.
(sit facing a partner, legs apart, holding hands; rock back and forth, as if rowing a boat)

Get out your binoculars,
What do you see?
(make two circles with the fingers on each hand, place at your eyes to create imaginary binoculars, and look around)

Oh no, I see an alligator!
Quick, row really fast!
(repeat song singing and rowing fast)

Repeat action and song with different speeds, as suggested by creature. If it's a friendly turtle or frog you see, row slowly. If it's a dangerous animal, row fast! Repeat song several times.

NATURE NOTES

Explore a puddle.

Use your binoculars to explore a puddle. Do you see anything moving? Do you see any worms nearby after the rainfall?

You'll be amazed at the creatures you can find near small puddles. You may see birds splashing in the puddle, using it as a refreshing birdbath. If the puddle is in the sun, draw a ring around it with a piece of chalk. Then, come back in a while and see if your puddle is becoming smaller, bigger, or staying the same size. What happened to the water?

If a grown-up is with you, perhaps you can visit a pond, where you may see a long-legged heron wading in the quiet water or a painted turtle basking on a rock in the sun. Take along a pair of real binoculars to help you spot more critters!

Note: Please watch any child near any amount of water, such as in a basin, wading pool, a puddle, or a pond.

 Let's Create

Easy Binoculars

When far away I want to see,
I look through binoculars made just for me!

WHAT YOU NEED

- Construction paper, cut into two 6" x 6" (15 x 15 cm) squares
- 2 toilet-paper tubes
- Glue stick
- Tape
- Hole punch
- Yarn
- Child-safety scissors
- Crayons

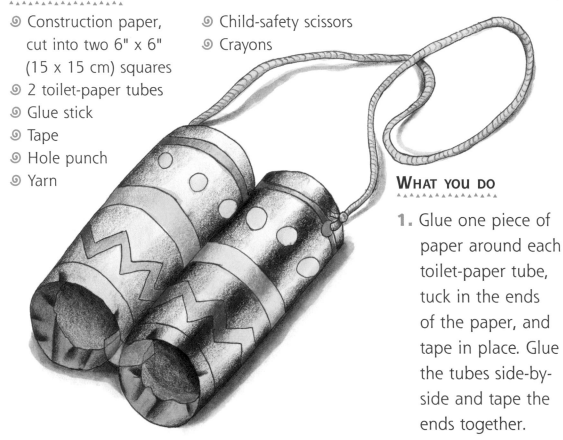

WHAT YOU DO

1. Glue one piece of paper around each toilet-paper tube, tuck in the ends of the paper, and tape in place. Glue the tubes side-by-side and tape the ends together.

2. Punch a hole in the end of each tube. Tie a piece of yarn to the binoculars so they can hang around your neck.

3. Use crayons to decorate your binoculars.

I spy Jake!

 Let's Play

We Spy...You!

The setup: Divide the group in half. Players stand side-by-side in two lines about 15 feet (5 m) apart.

The game: The first group secretly chooses the name of a person from the other line. Then they look through their pretend binoculars and chant "With my eyes, I spy (child's name)." The child called runs over and joins the chanting group's line. Now the other group looks through their binoculars and repeats the chant. Play continues until everyone has had a chance to switch lines at least one time.

 Let's Create

My Pond

WHAT YOU NEED

- Construction paper, one large sheet of green and scraps of other colors
- Child-safety scissors
- Markers

- Clear contact paper
- Stickers or drawings of pond animals or plants (fish, insects, frogs, ducks, turtles, weedy plants, and lily pads)
- Blue tissue paper

WHAT YOU DO

1. Fold a piece of green construction paper in half. Cut out the center. Open it up. Write "My Pond" on one side.

2. Ask a grown-up to help you cut two pieces of contact paper slightly larger than the pond paper. Peel off the backing from one of the contact sheets. Carefully smooth the pond paper border onto it, so that the writing faces down.

3. Arrange stickers of pond plants and animals face down onto the sticky contact paper. (Or, draw pond plants and animals on the construction paper scraps and cut them out.)

4. Cut a piece of blue tissue paper slightly bigger than the size of the pond opening. Carefully smooth it onto the sticker-covered contact paper.

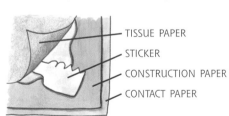

TISSUE PAPER
STICKER
CONSTRUCTION PAPER
CONTACT PAPER

5. Peel the backing from the second sheet of contact paper. Ask a grown-up to help you smooth it over the top of the pond art. (It helps to have one person hold one edge of the contact paper up, while another person begins to smooth the opposite edge onto the tissue paper.) Trim the edges.

6. Turn it all over to view your pond!

LITTLE HANDS Story Corner™

✽✽✽✽✽✽✽✽✽✽✽✽✽✽✽✽✽✽✽✽✽✽✽✽✽✽

Near One Cattail: Turtles, Logs and Leaping Frogs by Anthony D. Fredericks

Each Peach Pear Plum by Janet & Allan Ahlberg

Peek-a-Boo by Janet & Allan Ahlberg

I *Spy Little Learning Book* by Jean Marzollo

Froggy Fun

Frogs come in all sizes. Some frogs are smaller than a half-inch (1.25 cm) — smaller than a dime. Some frogs are as big as 10 inches (25 cm), almost as big as a ruler. The back feet of a frog are *webbed* to help them swim. Frogs also have short front legs and big, strong hind legs for jumping. Squat down low like a frog and see how far *you* can jump!

 Let's Sing

Ribbet, Ribbet

(Tune: "I'm a Little Teapot," or chant)

Ribbet, ribbet, ribbet,
Says the frog,
    (sit with legs in front, open and close fingers)

As it hops from log to log.
    (alternately slap the floor on either side of legs)

Ribbet, ribbet, ribbet,
Hippity-hop—
    (open and close fingers; slap hands on lap
    in rhythm)

Into the water with a
    (lift hands high, bend knees up)

Big kerplop!
    (spread knees and slap the floor)

Let's Draw

Look for the simple shapes in a jumping or swimming frog.

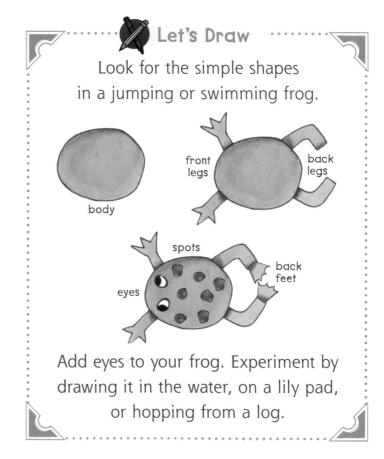

body

front legs

back legs

spots

eyes

back feet

Add eyes to your frog. Experiment by drawing it in the water, on a lily pad, or hopping from a log.

 Let's Play

Lily Pad Relay

The setup: Set two carpet squares 15 to 20 feet (5 to 7 m) apart. Line up evenly in two groups behind each square.

Place one lily pad (made from construction paper) on the ground in front of the player starting the relay. Give that player another lily pad to hold in her hand.

The game: The starting player begins by hopping onto the lily pad that is on the ground. She then sets the lily pad in her hand on the ground in front of her and hops onto it, then turns and picks up the lily pad that's now behind her. She continues racing to the opposite carpet square, stepping only on lily pads, and hands off the lily pad she's holding to the next person in line. Play continues until everyone has had a turn.

15 feet

It's a frog's (double) life.

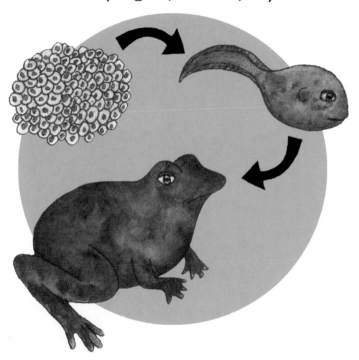

Frogs begin life as a tiny little egg in the water in a jelly-like mass with many other frog eggs. From the egg, a *tadpole* (also called a *polliwog*) hatches. The tadpole looks more like a fish than a frog. It has a tail and breathes through gills, just like a fish. As it grows, the tail disappears, legs grow for jumping and swimming, and those fishlike gills are replaced by lungs, so that the adult frog can breathe air — just like you do! Now the frog is ready to live on land. Frogs are *amphibians*, which means "double life," and it perfectly describes how they spend part of their lives on land and other times are in or near the water.

 Let's Create

Wide-Mouthed Frog Puppet

WHAT YOU NEED

- Child-safety scissors
- 2 paper plates, plus scraps of paper plates, card stock, or construction paper
- Stapler
- Green tempera paint, in a jar lid
- Paintbrush
- Marker
- Red construction paper scrap, 1" x 12" (2.5 x 30 cm)

step 1

step 3

step 4

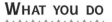

WHAT YOU DO

1. Cut the first paper plate in half. Fold the second paper plate in half. Staple each half plate to the back of the folded plate to create two pockets. Paint both sides green.

2. Cut two eyes from scrap paper. Fold the bottom of each eye, making a tab. Use a marker to draw eyeballs. Staple the eye tabs to the top pocket only.

3. Roll the red construction paper into a tongue. Insert it into the bottom of the mouth. Staple in place.

4. Put your fingers in the pockets to open and close your frog's mouth. Flick your wrist forward and see your frog stick its tongue out!

🖐 Let's Create

Pipe Cleaner Tree

WHAT YOU NEED

- ◎ Markers
- ◎ White card stock, or poster paper
- ◎ Child-safety scissors
- ◎ Pencil
- ◎ Pipe cleaners

Alongside most ponds, you will find cattails growing right along the edge, and further back, you will usually find a few trees growing.

WHAT YOU DO

1. Use markers to draw a tree-shape on card-stock paper. Color the tree. Then, cut it out.

2. Ask a grown-up to poke holes all over the treetop with a pencil.

3. Bend one end of a pipe cleaner. Starting on the back of the tree, stick the straight end of the pipe cleaner up through one of the holes. Lace it back down through a different hole.

4. Continue lacing it until you reach the pipe cleaner's end. Poke the end through to the back of the tree and bend it.

5. Repeat with more pipe cleaners.

Delicate Dragonfly

Dragonflies are beautiful, brightly colored insects. They have two pairs of very long wings that move separately, like a helicopter's blades. This allows the dragonfly to hover in one place, fly backward, and change directions at high speeds. Very clever!

Dragonflies are helpful insects that feed on harmful insects like mosquitoes, but don't munch on people. Hmmm. Would you rather have dragonflies or mosquitoes in your backyard?

Let's Create

Colorful Dragonfly

WHAT YOU NEED

- Glue stick
- Construction paper, 1 brightly colored sheet and 2 white sheets
- Paper-towel tube
- Child-safety scissors
- Markers
- Hole punch
- Pipe cleaner
- Tissue paper scraps
- Wiggly eyes

step 2

WHAT YOU DO

1. Glue the brightly colored construction paper around the paper-towel tube. Tuck in the ends of the paper.

2. Place the two white pieces of construction paper together. Draw and cut out wings.

3. Decorate the wings with markers. Glue the wings to the tube.

4. To make the antennae, use a hole punch to punch two holes in the end of the tube. Thread the pipe cleaner through the holes; fold the ends down.

5. To make the dragonfly's face, wad up a piece of tissue paper and stick it into the end of the tube. Glue wiggly eyes to the wadded paper.

6. Hold the dragonfly by the tail. Raise and lower it to make its wings flap. Sing the "DRAGONFLY" song (page 20).

Let's Draw

Look for the simple shapes in a dragonfly.

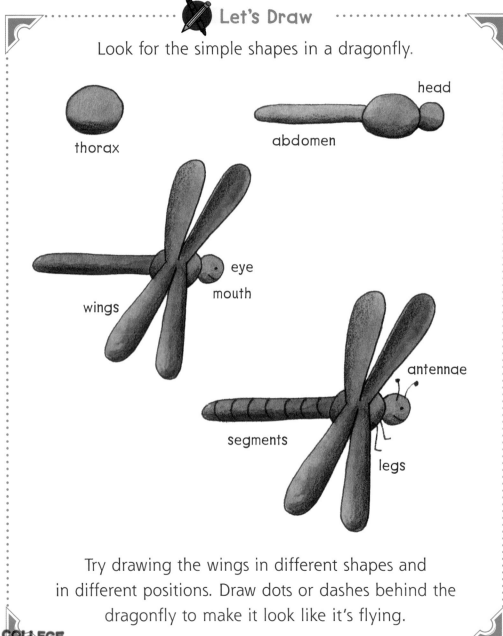

thorax

abdomen

head

wings

eye

mouth

segments

legs

antennae

Try drawing the wings in different shapes and in different positions. Draw dots or dashes behind the dragonfly to make it look like it's flying.

 **Let's Sing**

Dragonfly

(Tune: "Row, Row, Row Your Boat," or chant)

I'm a dragonfly,
Flying way up high.
> *(standing, flap your arms out to the side)*

Up and down,
> *(stretch both arms above head, then touch ground)*

Then turn around,
> *(turn around)*

Until I touch the ground.
> *(flap arms as you squat to the ground)*

Variation: Sitting, tuck arms
and flap elbows (lines 1 and 2),
reach arms above head then
touch the ground (line 3),
roll arms (line 4), touch the
ground (line 5).

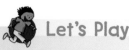 **Let's Play**

Dragonfly I Spy

The setup: Choose one person to be the Dragonfly. The Dragonfly stands in front of the group and secretly looks around to choose an object everyone will be able to see.

The game: The other players chant, "Dragonfly, dragonfly, what do you spy?" The Dragonfly responds by saying, "I spy something (insert descriptive words like "square," "blue," "tall," and so on). The other players take turns trying to guess what the item is. After several guesses the group can repeat the dragonfly chant to get another clue if necessary. Play continues until someone guesses the item and becomes the new Dragonfly.

Splish-Splash Fish!

What would a pond be without some fish? Not very fishy at all!

 Let's Sing

Ten Little Fishies in the Pond

(Tune: "Ten Little Indians," or chant)

One little, two little, three little fishies,
Four little, five little, six little fishies.
Seven little, eight little, nine little fishies,
Ten little fishies in the pond.
   (hold hands, walk in a circle while singing)

They jumped in the boat,
   (jump)

And the boat tipped over!
   (while holding hands, walk into the center of the circle)

They jumped in the boat,
   (jump)

And the boat tipped over!
   (while holding hands, walk out of the circle)

They jumped in the boat,
   (jump)

And the boat tipped over!
   (while holding hands, walk into the center of the circle)

Ten little fishies in the pond.
   (while holding hands, walk out of the circle)

NATURE NOTES

Fishy facts.

All fish have *fins*.
A fish moves its tail fin
so it can move through the
water. Fish use other fins to
steer and to stop. Some fish have
scales that cover their bodies, while
other fish have smooth, slimy skin.
Some fish have skeletons made of
bone, and other fish have skeletons
made of a tough, flexible material
called *cartilage*. You have bones
and cartilage in your body, too.
Feel the hard bones in your arms
and fingers. Now feel the flexible
cartilage in your nose. Don't
worry, you're not
part fish!

Let's Play

Fisherman Tag

The setup: Choose someone to be the Fisherman. Everyone else pretends to be a Fish swimming in the water.

The game: The Fisherman tries to catch a Fish by chasing and then tagging it. The first Fish caught becomes the new Fisherman.

Variation: When a Fish is caught it becomes a Fisherman along with the first Fisherman. The game continues until all the Fish have been caught and everyone has become a Fisherman.

Let's Draw

Fish come in all shapes and sizes.
Look for the simple shapes in these fish.

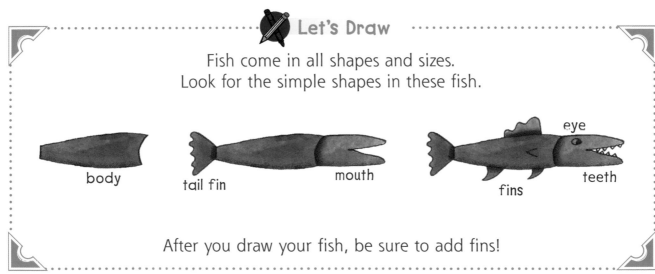

body

tail fin

mouth

eye

teeth

fins

After you draw your fish, be sure to add fins!

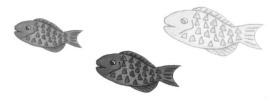

 Let's Sing

I'm Going Fishing

(Tune: "Three Little Ducks Went Out to Play," or chant)

I'm going fishing,
(pretend to hold a fishing pole, resting it on your shoulder)

With my fishing pole.
(bring hands forward as you pretend to cast)

Down by the water,
At the fishing hole.
(make a circle with your arms out front)

I see the little fishies,
(palms together, wiggle hands as if they are a fish)

Splashing about.
I beg and I plead,
(hold hands, palms up, arms outstretched)

"Won't you please come out?"
(cup hands and clap together on the word "out")

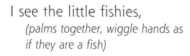

LITTLE HANDS Story Corner™

Piggy and Dad Go Fishing by David Martin

Three Wishes by Harriet Ziefert

Fish Eyes: A Book You Can Count On by Lois Ehlert

Fish! by Christopher Nicholas

Fish on a Fishing Pole

WHAT YOU NEED

- Child-safety scissors
- Card-stock paper
- Construction paper, various colors
- Glue
- Hole punch
- Plastic drinking straw
- Yarn, a piece about 1 foot (30 cm) long

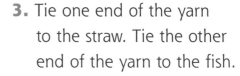

WHAT YOU DO

1. Cut a large fish from card-stock paper. Tear colored construction paper into small pieces. Glue them onto your fish to create colorful scales. Cut eyes from black construction paper. Glue them onto your fish.

2. Use a hole punch to make a hole near the fish's mouth. Make another hole in one end of the straw.

3. Tie one end of the yarn to the straw. Tie the other end of the yarn to the fish.

4. Sing "I'M GOING FISHING" (page 23) while playing with your new fishing pole.

Terrific Turtle

NATURE NOTES

Peek-a-Boo!

Who? A turtle, of course. Most turtles can tuck their head and limbs inside their shell for protection. A turtle's shell is actually part of its skeleton. And just like your skeleton, a turtle can never take its shell off. Pretend that your shirt is your shell. Pull your head inside just like a turtle does. Notice how your eyes and neck are now protected.

 Let's Sing

I'm a Little Turtle

(Tune: "I'm a Little Teapot," or chant)

Just for fun, draw a turtle's face on your thumb before you sing this turtle song.

I'm a little turtle,
  (make a fist with thumb out; place other hand on top for the turtle's shell)

Traveling all around.
I wear a hard shell,
  (wiggle thumb [turtle's head] in rhythm)

And walk on the ground.

I'm a little turtle,
Going so slow.
I tuck in my head,
  (tuck thumb into fist)

Then POP!
  (pop thumb out)

Off I go.
  (wiggle thumb [turtle's head] in rhythm)

 Let's Create

Turtle Puppet

WHAT YOU NEED

- 2 small paper plates
- Child-safety scissors
- Markers
- Green or brown construction paper scraps
- Glue (optional)
- Stapler
- 2 plastic drinking straws
- Tape

step 1

step 3

FOLDED STRAW

step 4

WHAT YOU DO

1. Place the paper plates together with the tops facing each other. Cut a small notch about one inch (2.5 cm) wide for the turtle's tail.

2. Use markers to color the bottom sides of the plates, making one plate the top shell, and the other plate the bottom shell. Glue pieces of torn construction paper to the top shell to make a pattern, if desired.

3. Cut the turtle's head and legs from green or brown construction paper. Staple the legs to the top side of the bottom shell.

4. Staple the head to one end of the first straw. Fold the second straw in half around the first straw, just below the turtle's head. (This keeps the head from coming completely out of the shell.) Wrap straws with tape to hold in place.

5. Place the straw between the two plates, with the head between the front two legs, and the end of the straw coming out of the notch. Staple the plates together on either side of the notch.

6. Pull the head back so that the widest part of the face is at the rim of the plates. Staple on either side of the head, but not on the head itself.

7. Make your turtle tuck its head in and out by gently pushing and pulling the straw. Sing "I'M A LITTLE TURTLE" (page 25) as you move your puppet.

LITTLE HANDS Story Corner™

Yertle the Turtle by Dr. Seuss

Old Turtle by Douglas Wood

Turtle and Snake Go Camping by Kate Spohn

Let's Play

Turtle Shell Relay

The setup: Set two carpet squares 15 to 20 feet (5 to 7 m) apart. Line up evenly, in groups of two, behind each of the carpet squares.

The game: The first pair in line steps into a hula hoop. They pull the hoop up around their middles and race to the other carpet square. Then they drop the hoop to the ground and step out of it. The waiting pair then steps in and continues the race. Play until everyone has had a turn.

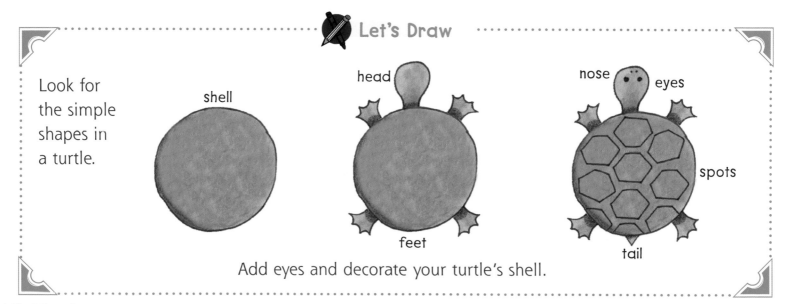

Let's Draw

Look for the simple shapes in a turtle.

shell

head

feet

nose   eyes

spots

tail

Add eyes and decorate your turtle's shell.

Quack, Quack, Quack!

 **Let's Sing**

Quack, Quack Went the Little Yellow Duck

(Tune: "Gung, Gung, Went the Little Green Frog," or chant)

"Quack, quack,"
(open and close hand)

Went the little yellow duck one day.
(tuck hands and flap wings)

"Quack, quack,"

Went the little yellow duck.
(repeat actions above)

"Quack, quack,"
Went the little yellow duck one day.
(repeat actions above)

And his feet went,
Flip, flap, flop.
*(hands side by side, palms down,
alternately slap lap with hands)*

NATURE NOTES

Duck walk.

Ducks like to swim in ponds or streams. They have webbed feet that they use like paddles to help them swim. Have you ever gone swimming with flippers or fins on your feet? It sure makes swimming easier, doesn't it! Walking on land isn't quite as easy for ducks. Those big webbed feet get in the way!

That's why ducks waddle side to side when they walk. Put on fins or flippers and try to walk. Be careful; it's not easy!

Ask a grown-up if you can visit a park with a pond and ducks. Take breadcrumbs to feed them, if permitted at the park. Do all of the ducks look and act the same? Do they seem more comfortable *in* the water or *out* of the water?

Waddling Duck

WHAT YOU NEED

- Pencil
- 4 large paper plates
- Child-safety scissors
- 1 small paper plate
- Stapler
- Markers, paint and paintbrush, or glue and construction paper

step 1

CUT SLIT

step 2

step 3

WHAT YOU DO

1. Draw a duck's head on one large paper plate and cut it out. Fold the second paper plate in half. Cut out two webbed feet.

2. Fold the last two large plates in half. Cut a slit on the fold of the plates long enough for the duck's head to slide in, about 2 1/2 inches (6 cm). Fold the small paper plate in thirds. Staple the duck's feet to the center of the small plate.

3. Staple the small plate to one of the plates with a slit. Slide the duck's head into the other plate with a slit; staple in place.

4. Set the plate with the head on top of the duck base and pull it slightly forward. Staple the plates together at the back of the duck's neck.

5. Decorate your duck by coloring it with markers, painting it, or gluing on feathers cut from construction paper. You could even try a mixture of all three!

Let's Draw

Look for the simple shapes in a duck.

body

head

eye and beak

wing

legs

feet

LITTLE HANDS
Story Corner™

Little White Duck by Walt Whippo

Duck, Duck, Goose! (A Coyote's on the Loose!) by Karen Beaumont

Five Little Ducks by Raffi

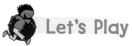 Let's Play

Duck, Duck, Goose

DUCK...
DUCK...
GOOSE!

The setup: All players sit down in a circle facing each other. One person is chosen to be "It."

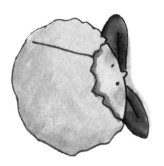

The game: The player who is "It" walks around the circle, tapping each player's head and saying either "duck" or "goose." "Ducks" stay seated. But if "goose" is said, that player must get up and try to chase "It" around the circle. The goal is to tap "It" before she reaches the Goose's seat and sits down. Once both the Goose and "It" return to the place where the Goose was sitting, both sit down. Repeat the game until everyone has had a chance to chase and/or be chased.

It's a Snap!

 Let's Sing

Chomp, Chomp Went the Little Green Alligator

(Tune: "Gung, Gung, Went the Little Green Frog," or chant)

Chomp, chomp,
Went the little green alligator.
(arms straight, clap hands together twice; then clasp hands, wiggle side to side)

Chomp, chomp,
Went the little green gator.
(repeat actions)

Chomp, chomp,
Went the little green alligator.
(repeat actions)

And its tail went,
Swish, swish, swish.
(clap palms together sideways, swish arms side to side)

NATURE NOTES

Alligator Alert!

Alligators spend most of their lives in the water. Their nostrils and eyes are located on top of their snout. This allows them to keep their body hidden beneath the water as they lay waiting for their next meal. Snap!

Snapping Alligator

Alligators have very powerful jaws filled with lots of teeth. They grow new teeth throughout their lives. As their old teeth break or become dull, they fall out and are replaced by new ones. An alligator can have hundreds — even thousands — of teeth in its lifetime. Imagine all *that* brushing!

WHAT YOU NEED

- 2 paper plates
- Child-safety scissors
- Red, green, and black markers
- Stapler
- Paper plate scraps or construction paper
- Tape

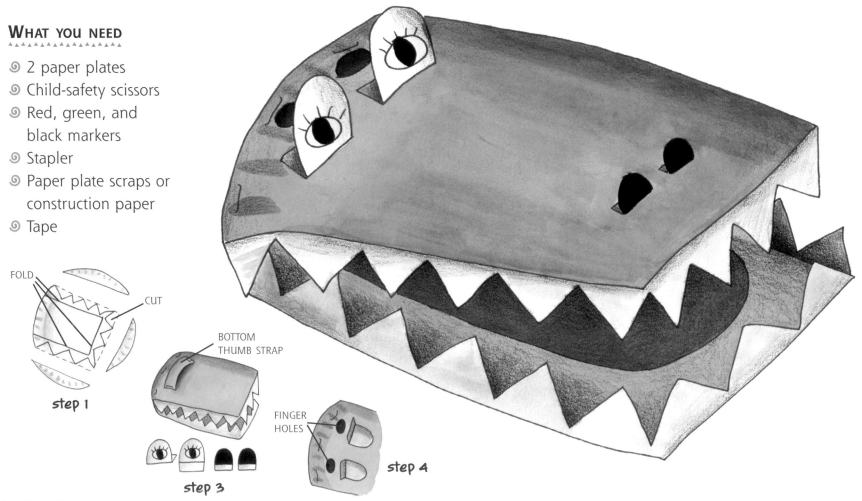

FOLD

CUT

step 1

BOTTOM THUMB STRAP

step 3

FINGER HOLES

step 4

WHAT YOU DO

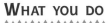

1. Place two paper plates on top of each other. Fold three edges of the plates down to create the alligator's head. Leaving about one inch (2.5 cm) on the outside of the fold for the alligator's teeth, trim the rounded edges off. Cut triangles to make teeth.

2. Separate the plates. Color the top plate green (both sides) for the top snout. Use a red marker to draw a tongue on the top side of the other plate. Color the rest of the bottom snout (both sides) green. Staple the top and bottom snouts together. Fold the teeth down.

3. Using paper plate scraps, cut a strip 1" x 4" (2.5 x 10 cm) and staple it to the bottom snout. Color the strip green. Cut eyes and nostrils from other paper scraps. Fold the bottom flaps under. Draw eyeballs and color the nostrils. Tape the eyes and nostrils to the top snout.

4. Ask a grown-up to cut two finger holes in the top snout, behind the eyes. Place your middle finger on top, and put two fingers into the holes. Place your thumb in the bottom thumb strap. Open and close your fingers to watch your alligator snap! Repeat the "HUNGRY LITTLE ALLIGATOR" chant with your puppet.

 Let's Sing

Hungry Little Alligator

(Chant)

Hungry little alligator,
(clasp hands together like an alligator's snout)

Looking for its lunch.
(wiggle hands side to side)

Sees a little fish,
Then crunch, crunch, crunch!
(arms straight, clap hands three times)

Have fun with this chant. What will the alligator eat next? A great big hamburger, a red tomato, a hippopotamus, or a house?

Alligator Chomp

Rats! I mean . . . gators!

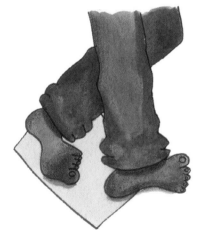

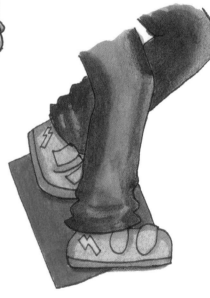

The setup: Get one piece of construction paper for every player. Draw a big alligator on one of the pieces of paper. Stand in a circle with each person standing on one of the pieces of construction paper. Set a kitchen timer for less than a minute.

The game: Everyone begins walking in a circle stepping on each of the pieces of paper. Try not to be the one standing on the alligator when the timer goes off!

Variations: Sit in a circle and pass a stuffed animal (or a folded pair of socks). Try not to be holding the "alligator" when the timer goes off. If you don't have a timer, play music. Someone stands with his back to the group playing the music. When the music is turned off, the person holding the "alligator" will be in charge of playing the music during the next round.

In My Garden

In my garden, it's as pleasant as can be,
With butterflies, ladybugs, and bumblebees.

Plant a garden or make a flower,
Use your fingers to create rain showers.

Wriggle like a caterpillar, or be a butterfly,
Soar like a bird way up high in the sky.

Come into my garden and you will see,
Just how much fun a garden can be.

My Garden

 Let's Create

My Mini Greenhouse

In my greenhouse, rain or snow,
I plant a seed and watch it grow!

WHAT YOU NEED

- 2 paper plates
- Child-safety scissors
- Stapler
- Markers
- 3 cotton balls
- Plastic zip-locking sandwich bag
- Bean, sunflower, or pumpkin seeds
- Yarn

LITTLE HANDS Story Corner™

Oh Say Can You Seed? All About Flowering Plants by Bonnie Worth

How Groundhog's Garden Grew by Lynne Cherry

How Are You Peeling? Foods with Moods by Saxton Freymann and Joost Elffers

step 1

FOLD BACK

step 2

step 3

step 5

WHAT YOU DO

1. Place the two paper plates together. Cut them into a greenhouse shape. Ask a grown-up to help you cut a rectangle out of the center.

2. With the bottoms of the plates still together and facing you, fold the tops and bottoms back. Then, separate the plates and turn them so that the bottoms of the plates are facing each other. Staple the top flaps together.

3. Flip the greenhouse so that the stapled flaps are on the inside. Decorate the outside with markers.

4. Dip three cotton balls in water; gently squeeze out the excess water. Place the cotton balls into the zip-locking bag. Add two to three seeds and seal the bag.

5. Open the greenhouse. Roll the top of the bag so that the seeds will show through the greenhouse window. Staple the bag to the folded-down top flaps.

6. Close your greenhouse. Overlap the bottom flaps slightly and staple. The greenhouse should now be able to stand upright. Tie a piece of yarn through your greenhouse for a handle.

Now, set your greenhouse in indirect sunlight and watch your seeds grow! When they get too big for the bag, remove them gently from the bag and plant them in soil.

NATURE NOTES

Got green thumbs?

Someone who is good at growing plants is said to have a "green thumb." But that doesn't mean the person's thumb is really green. It's a friendly way of saying that person is able to take care of plants and help them to grow well. Do you or someone you know have a green thumb?

MORE FUN

Do a leaf rubbing. Place a leaf on a smooth, hard surface, such as a table. Put a piece of paper on top of the leaf. Use a crayon to color back and forth over the entire leaf. Watch as the shape and texture of the leaf magically appear on your paper! How did that happen?

 **Let's Sing**

This Is the Way We Plant Our Garden

(Tune: "Here We Go 'Round the Mulberry Bush," or chant)

This is the way we plant our garden,
(hold hands and walk in a circle)

Plant our garden,

Plant our garden.

This is the way we plant our garden,

So early in the morning.

Continue with more verses: Rake *(pretend to rake)*, dig a hole *(pretend to dig)*, plant the seeds *(jump up and down)*, water our garden *(hold hands, go in and out)*, watch it grow *(bend down then jump up high)*, then repeat the first verse.

 Let's Draw

Many plants have leaves. Leaves come in different shapes and sizes.
Look for the simple shapes in these leaves.

Draw the leaves, using the shapes you see. Add details like *veins* on the leaf and *texture* to the edges of the leaf. Are these green spring leaves or are they red and yellow leaves of autumn?

In Full Bloom

NATURE NOTES

See a flower, see a seed.

When a plant produces a flower it is said to be "blooming." The flower on a plant often looks and smells beautiful, but also it has a very important job. The flower is the part of the plant that produces *seeds*. The seeds enable the plant to reproduce and make new plants.

Look at the flower of a dandelion plant. As it ages, or ripens, the flower develops into feathery white seed tufts. When the wind blows, the seeds are carried away. If you find a dandelion with seed tufts, blow on it to see how the seeds spread in the wind. If you find one with a yellow flower, pull the yellow petals out to find the developing seeds at the ends of the petals.

 Let's Sing

Seeds to Flowers

(Tune: "Mary Had a Little Lamb," or chant)

Spring has brought us sun
(standing, arch hands over head)

And showers.
(rain fingers down)

Sun and showers,
(arch hands over head, rain fingers down)

Sun and showers.
(repeat action)

Spring has brought us sun
(arch hands over head)

And showers.
(rain fingers down to the ground)

So seeds
(squat into a ball)

Will grow and
(slowly roll up to standing)

Turn to flowers.
(spread arms and legs)

🖐 Let's Create
Pretty Flower

WHAT YOU NEED

- 1 small paper plate
- Child-safety scissors
- Froot Loops or other colorful cereal rings
- Glue
- Paintbrush (optional)
- Tape
- Colored craft sticks or Popsicle sticks

step 1

WHAT YOU DO

1. Cut a small paper plate into a flower shape. Glue cereal rings onto the plate. (Younger artists may want to paint the glue onto the plate and then add the cereal rings.)

2. Tape a craft stick to the back of your flower for the stem.

3. To add leaves, ask a grown-up to cut another craft stick in half. Glue the leaves to the stem.

 Let's Play

Picking Flowers

The setup: Choose one person to be "It." Everyone else sits in a circle.

The game: The person chosen to be "It" begins by walking on the outside of the circle carrying a plastic flower, scarf, or sock. Everyone sings:

I'm Picking Flowers

(Tune: "Skip to My Lou," or chant)

I'm picking flowers, yes I am.
I'm picking flowers, yes I am.
I'm picking flowers, yes I am.
I'm picking flowers, and I pick ... YOU!

The player who is "It" drops the flower behind one of the sitting players. That person picks up the flower and chases "It" around the outside of the circle. When "It" reaches the empty spot in the circle, she sits down. If the Chaser tags "It" before she sits down, then "It" takes another turn being "It." Otherwise, the Chaser becomes "It."

Repeat the song until everyone has had a chance to chase and be chased.

YOU!!!

MORE FUN

Year-'round Flower Power

Place a flower or two (separate the two flowers for best results) between two paper towels. Set the paper towels between several sheets of newspaper. Now, stack heavy books on top of the newspaper. Leave the flower there for several days until it is dry. Glue the dried flower onto a folded piece of construction paper to make a card or cut out a long strip of paper to use as a bookmark. Glue the flower to the bookmark.

 Let's Draw

The petals of a flower are usually its prettiest and most fragrant part. They help attract birds and insects to the flower. Petals come in many different shapes and sizes. Look for the simple shapes in these flowers.

Experiment with different petal shapes, different leaf shapes, and different colors. Then, draw a garden with lots of different flowers in it.

Big Bumblebee

 Let's Sing

Buzzing Little Bees

(Tune: "Little Tommy Thumbkin or Little Bunny Foo-Foo," or chant)

Buzzing little bees,
(hold wrist with one hand, wiggle fingers)

Closed up in the hive.
(slide hand up over bent fingers)

It's time to get to work now, 1-2-3-4-5.
(pop fingers out one at a time)

Bzzzzzzzzzz!
(wiggle fingers all around)

Gathered all your pollen,
(wiggle fingers all around)

Now your work is done.
Back inside the hive you go,
(hold wrist with one hand, wiggle fingers)

5-4-3-2-1
(starting with thumb, fold one finger down at a time)

Bzzzzzzzzzz!
(slide hand up over bent fingers)

NATURE NOTES

Pollen Patrol!

Bees have a very important job of spreading *pollen* from flower to flower so that plants can make fruits and seeds. When a bee lands on a flower to collect nectar for making honey, the pollen in the flower sticks to its legs. When the bee lands on another flower, some of the pollen from the first flower is left behind. But the funny thing is, the bee doesn't even know it is helping out!

✏️ Let's Draw

Look for the simple shapes in a bee.

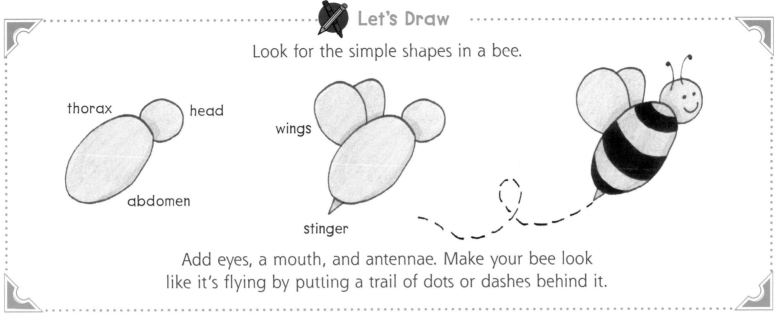

thorax head

abdomen

wings

stinger

Add eyes, a mouth, and antennae. Make your bee look
like it's flying by putting a trail of dots or dashes behind it.

 Let's Play

Buzzing Bees Game

The setup: Choose one person to be the Bee. (Large
groups may want to choose more than one Bee.)
Everyone else is a Flower. All of the Flowers tuck the
end of a scarf, sock, or washcloth (pollen) into the
waist of their pants.

The game: The Flowers scatter (run) as the Bee tries
to catch up with them and gather their pollen by
grabbing their scarves. The last flower to have its
pollen gathered by the Bee will become the new Bee.

BZZZZZZ

Big Round Bumblebee

WHAT YOU NEED

- Child-safety scissors
- 5 paper plates
- Yellow and black tempera paint, in separate jar lids
- Paintbrushes
- Hole punch
- Yarn, cut about 3 feet (1 m) long
- Tape
- Newspaper or scrap paper
- Stapler
- Glue stick

step 1

step 4

step 6

WHAT YOU DO

1. To create the bee's head, cut the center circle from one paper plate. Paint it yellow. Let dry. Paint the bee's face on the small yellow circle with black paint.

2. Paint the bottom of two other paper plates yellow. Let dry. Paint black stripes.

3. Cut two antennae and a stinger from the plate scraps. Paint them black.

4. With the painted sides out, put the two striped plates together. Punch holes around the outside rims. Tie one end of the yarn to the plates. Wrap a piece of tape around the other end to create a dull needle. Lace the plates together, leaving an opening.

5. Stuff the plates with wadded-up newspaper. Then finish lacing and tie a knot.

6. Cut the last two plates in half. Round off the ends to make wings. Spread the wings slightly and staple them together in pairs.

7. Staple both sets of wings to the bee's body. Staple the stinger to the bottom of the body. Tape or staple the antennae to the bee's head. Glue the bee's head to the front of its body.

LITTLE HANDS
Story Corner™

Whose House? by Barbara Seuling

Buzz Said the Bee by Wendy Cheyette Lewison

Honey in a Hive by Anne Rockwell

Lucky Ladybug

I f you find a ladybug in your garden, consider yourself lucky!
Ladybugs eat lots of insects that are harmful to plants!

 Let's Create

Hanging Ladybug

WHAT YOU NEED

- 1 small paper plate
- Red, black, and white tempera paints, in seperate jar lids
- Paintbrushes
- Yarn
- Stapler
- Pencil
- Black construction paper
- Child-safety scissors
- Pipe cleaner (¹/₃ per puppet)
- Tape

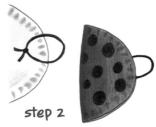

step 2

step 3

step 4

WHAT YOU DO

1. Paint the bottom of a small paper plate red. Let dry. Paint black spots. Let dry.

2. Tie a piece of yarn in a loop for hanging. Fold the paper plate in half around the yarn. Staple the plate closed.

3. To make the ladybug's head, fold a piece of black construction paper in half. Draw the head so the bottom is on the fold. Cut out the head,

making sure that you don't cut on the fold. Use white paint to add eyes and a mouth.

4. Shape the pipe cleaner into antennae, folding the ends down. Tape the antennae to the inside of the head. Slide the plate inside the head. Staple it in place.

5. Cut three pieces of yarn for legs. Fold each piece in half. Tape the legs to the back of the ladybug.

Let's Draw

Look for the simple shapes in this ladybug.

Add eyes, antennae, and legs. Draw spots on your ladybug.

 Let's Play

Pin the Spots on the Ladybug

A ladybug's real name is a "ladybird beetle." Ladybirds are brightly colored with dome-shaped bodies. They are commonly red, yellow, or orange. They usually have black, white, or yellow spots. Play this game with a ladybird's spots!

The setup: Hang a large ladybug (ladybird), made from paper, on the wall. Line up 10 to 15 feet (3 to 5 m) away. Give everyone a paper ladybug spot with tape attached.

The game: The first person in line runs to the ladybug and attaches her spot to it. Then she runs back and the next person in line goes. The race continues until the ladybug has all of its spots.

Variation: For even more fun, play in turns with a blindfold on. Spin the blindfolded player gently and then set her off toward the wall.

LITTLE HANDS Story Corner™

Five Little Ladybugs by Melanie Gerth

The Grouchy Ladybug by Eric Carle

Backyard Detective: Critters Up Close by Nic Bishop

 Let's Sing

The Itsy Bitsy Ladybug

(Tune: "The Itsy Bitsy Spider," or chant)

The itsy bitsy ladybug,
Crawled up the waterspout.
(alternately walk thumbs to pointer fingers, starting low then walking up high)

Down came the rain,
(fingers on both hands rain down)

And washed the ladybug out.
(cross arms in front and swish out)

Out came the sun,
(arch arms overhead)

And dried up all the rain.
(bring arms down to sides)

And the itsy bitsy ladybug,
(alternate walking thumbs to pointer fingers, low then high)

Went up the spout again.

Crawly Caterpillar

 Let's Sing

Creepy, Crawly Caterpillar

(Tune: "The Wheels on the Bus," or chant)

Creepy, crawly caterpillar,
   (bend and straighten index finger)

Munch, munch, munch.
   (open and close hand)

Munch, munch, munch.
Munch, munch, munch.
Creepy, crawly caterpillar,
   (bend and straighten index finger)

Munch, munch, munch.
   (open and close hand)

All it eats are leaves for lunch.

Creepy, crawly caterpillar,
   (bend and straighten index finger)

Spins a cozy bed.
   (roll arms)

Spins a cozy bed.
Spins a cozy bed.
Creepy crawly caterpillar,
   (bend and straighten index finger)

Spins a cozy bed.
   (roll arms)

Where it lays and rests its head.
   (lay head on hands like sleeping)

Creepy, crawly caterpillar,
   (bend and straighten index finger)

Opens up its eyes.
   (point to both eyes, lean head side to side)

Opens up its eyes.
Opens up its eyes.
Creepy crawly caterpillar,
   (bend and straighten index finger)

Opens up its eyes.
   (point to both eyes, lean head side to side)

Now with wings, oh, what a surprise!
   (slowly spread arms out in surprise)

Creepy, crawly caterpillar,
   (bend and straighten index finger)

Now a butterfly.
   (spread arms and flap)

Now a butterfly.
Now a butterfly.
Creepy crawly caterpillar,
   (bend and straighten index finger)

Now a butterfly.
   (spread arms and flap)

Spreads its wings and flies through the sky.

NATURE NOTES

The caterpillar's journey

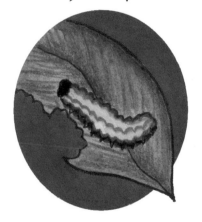

A baby butterfly is called a *caterpillar*. A caterpillar doesn't have any wings. It looks more like a worm than a butterfly. The baby caterpillar will have to grow and undergo a major *transformation* (change) before it looks like its parents. This change is called *metamorphosis*. It's a very exciting time for a caterpillar!

Wriggly Caterpillar

WHAT YOU NEED

- 2 toilet-paper tubes, each cut into 3 segments
- Hole punch
- Tape
- Yarn, 12 inches (30 cm) long
- Pipe cleaner
- Wiggly eyes
- Glue
- Markers

step 1

step 2

step 3

WHAT YOU DO

1. To create the middle segments, use a hole-punch to punch two holes *straight across from each other*, in four of the tube segments.

2. To create the caterpillar's ends, use a hole-punch to punch two holes *next to each other* in the last two tube segments.

3. Wrap a piece of tape around one end of the yarn to make a needle. Lace the yarn through one of the end tubes and tie a knot. Add the four middle tubes. Lace through the last end tube and tie another knot.

4. To make the head, punch two holes in the top of one end segment. Thread a 4-inch (10 cm) piece of pipe cleaner through the two holes. Bend the ends down to form antennae. Glue wiggly eyes to the face. Use markers to decorate your caterpillar.

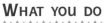 

 Let's Play

Hungry, Hungry Caterpillar

When a caterpillar hatches from its egg, it has an enormous appetite. It eats, and eats, and eats! When it gets too big for its own skin, its skin splits open. The caterpillar crawls out wearing a brand-new skin!

The setup: Make lots of little leaves from construction paper. Toss the leaves around the room.

The game: Race to see who can gobble up (hold in hand) the most leaves.

Variation: Players make 10 leaves each. Write your name on your leaves, or use different colored leaves for each person. Mix the leaves together. Spread them around the room. Race to find all 10 of your leaves.

LITTLE HANDS
Story Corner™

The Very Hungry Caterpillar by Eric Carle

Caterpillar Dance by Scott Mcbee

Waiting for Wings by Lois Ehlert

Monarch Butterflies by Lynn Rosenblatt

Beautiful Butterfly

Butterfly, butterfly as pretty as can be,
Spread your wings for all to see!

 Let's Play

Caterpillar-Butterfly Race

Set two carpet squares 10 to 15 feet (3 to 5 m) apart. Line up behind one of the squares. Crawl like a caterpillar to the opposite carpet square, then come back flying like a butterfly!

NATURE NOTES

Butter flies!

How did the butterfly get its name? Some think it came from a common European butterfly called the *yellow brimstone*. At first people called it the "butter-colored fly." The name was then shortened to "butterfly."

LITTLE HANDS Story Corner™

The Lamb and the Butterfly by Arnold Sundgaard

The Butterfly House by Eve Bunting

The Butterfly Alphabet by Kjell B. Sandved

Butterflies by Karen Shapiro

 Let's Sing

The Butterfly Chant

(Tune: "I'm a Little Teapot," or chant)

Once I was a caterpillar,
(bend and straighten index finger)

Crawling on the ground.
Now I'm a butterfly,
(cross hands, hook thumbs together)

Fluttering all around!
(flap fingers back and forth)

 Let's Create

Butterfly Ring

WHAT YOU NEED

- Child-safety scissors
- Construction paper or tissue-paper scraps
- Plastic sandwich bag
- Pipe cleaner, cut in half

step 3

WHAT YOU DO

1. Cut, tear, or wad colorful construction paper or tissue-paper scraps into small pieces. Put the pieces into a sandwich bag with half of the scraps on each side of the bag. Close the bag and gather it at the center.

2. Cut a pipe cleaner in half. Twist one half into a ring big enough to fit around your finger. Cut off the excess pipe cleaner. Bend any pointed ends so that they won't poke out.

3. Thread the second half of the pipe cleaner through the ring. Then place it on the gather of the bag, wrap it around, and twist it to hold.

4. Bend the tips of the pipe cleaner to form the butterfly's antennae. Slip the ring onto your finger. Wiggle your hand to make your butterfly fly!

Variation: Fill your butterfly with colorful cereal or candies and use it as a party favor!

 Let's Play

Butterfly, Butterfly, Turn Around

(Tune: "Teddy Bear, Teddy Bear," or chant)

Did you know that a butterfly tastes with its feet? This saves it time and energy.
As soon as the butterfly touches something with its feet, it can tell whether or not it
is worth taking the time to land and begin searching for nectar. Imagine what life
would be like if you could taste with *your* feet as you do this action rhyme!

To play: Stand in a big circle
wearing your butterfly ring. Repeat
the following chant doing each of
the movements with your BUTTERFLY
RING (page 55):

Butterfly, butterfly turn around.
(turn around)

Butterfly, butterfly touch the ground.
(touch the ground)

Butterfly, butterfly way up high.
(reach up high)

Butterfly, butterfly, fly, fly, fly.
(flap your hand up and down)

Butterfly, butterfly touch my toes.
(touch your toes)

Butterfly, butterfly touch my nose.
(touch your nose)

Butterfly, butterfly so pretty to see.
(flap your hand up and down)

Butterfly, butterfly touch my knee.
(touch your knee)

Butterfly, butterfly in the sky.
(flap your hand up and down)

Butterfly, butterfly touch my thigh.
(touch your thigh)

Butterfly, butterfly, touch my head.
(touch your head)

Butterfly, butterfly off to bed.
(fly butterfly behind your back)

Variation: Take turns being the leader
and telling all of the other butterflies
what to do. Start with one command,
then get trickier by combining two or
three commands *(touch your toes,
knees, AND nose).*

Feathered Friends

Birds are the only animals that have feathers. Feathers help protect the birds' skin and keep it dry. A bird fluffs its feathers up to keep warm or holds them close to its body to keep cool. And, of course, feathers help some birds to fly!

NATURE NOTES

Nice nest.

Help a bird build a warm and cozy nest by supplying it with building materials. Gather soft materials such as dryer lint, dog hair, pieces of yarn, and ribbon. Leave them in bushes or trees where birds can find them. Some day you might just find an unusual nest made from those same materials!

 Let's Play

Birds in the Nest

The setup: Choose one person to be the Mother (or Father) Bird. All other players will be Baby Birds. Choose a place to be the nest.

The game: Start with all of the Baby Birds flying around out of the nest. The Mother (or Father) Bird has to chase all the Baby Birds and bring them back to the nest. The last bird caught gets to be the next Mother (or Father) bird.

 Let's Sing

My Little House Up on a Hill

(Tune: "Hush, Little Baby," or chant)

My little house up on the hill,
(make a roof over your head)

Baby bird on my windowsill.
(tuck hands under arms and flap wings)

Looking for a cozy nest,
(cup hands)

Where he'll take a nice long rest.
(rest head on hands)

Flying Birds

WHAT YOU NEED

- Pencil
- Construction paper
- Child-safety scissors
- Glue stick
- Markers
- Hole punch and yarn, or craft or Popsicle stick

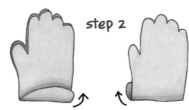

step 2

WHAT YOU DO

1. Trace your foot on a piece of construction paper. Fold another piece of paper in half and trace your handprint. Cut them out.

2. Keeping your handprints together, put a crease in the palm. Then separate the handprints, and reverse the direction of the fold on one of them.

3. Put glue on the bottom fold of one of the handprints. Attach it to your footprint. Turn your bird over and repeat the process with the other handprint.

4. Fold another piece of construction paper in half and cut out two beaks. Glue one beak to each side of the bird. Use markers to add eyes and other decorations.

5. Decide if you want your bird to hang from the ceiling or to be a stick puppet.

To hang your bird: Hold the bird with two fingers behind the wings to find the best balancing point. Then punch a hole behind the wings. Attach a piece of yarn.

For a stick puppet: Glue a craft stick to one side of the bird, just behind the wing. Wave your bird back and forth to see its wings flap.

Let's Draw

Look for the simple shapes in this standing bird.

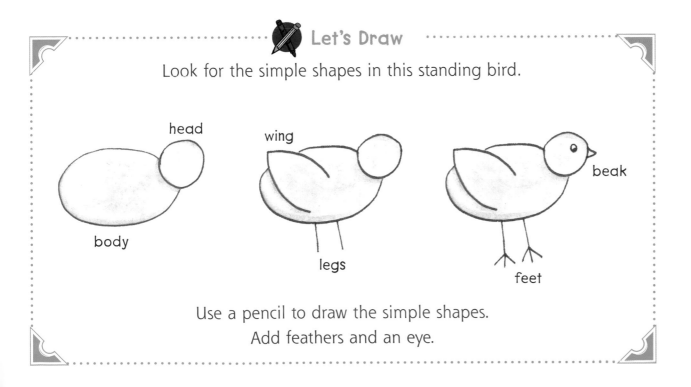

head
wing
beak
body
legs
feet

Use a pencil to draw the simple shapes.
Add feathers and an eye.

LITTLE HANDS
Story Corner™

Birds Build Nests
by Yvonne Winer

Bird Tales from Near and Far
by Susan Milord

Slowpoke Snail

Snails are one of nature's biggest slowpokes. They move very s-l-o-w-l-y, gliding along on a large flattened "foot." Look for signs of snails in and around your garden. Can you spot leaves, fruits, and vegetables with bites taken out of them? Can you see slimy trails on sidewalks around the garden? If so, you just might have snails around!

Let's Create

Sliding Snail

WHAT YOU NEED

- Stapler
- 2 paper plates
- Black marker
- Child-safety scissors
- Tissue paper (assorted colors)
- Paintbrush
- Glue
- Construction paper

step 1

step 3

WHAT YOU DO

1. Staple two plates together with the tops facing each other. Fold the bottoms of the plates inward. Use a marker to draw a spiral on the front "shell" (plate).

2. Cut tissue paper into squares. Paint glue onto the shell and add tissue paper squares. For a shiny shell, paint a layer of glue on top of the tissue paper. Let it dry.

3. Cut the snail's head and foot from construction paper. Staple them to the inside of the front shell. Draw a face on the snail's head.

4. Spread the bottom of the plates apart to make your snail stand up.

Snail City by Jane O'Connor

Snappy Little Bugs: See the Bugs Jump, Hop, and Crawl by Derek Matthews

The Little Hands Nature Book by Nancy Castaldo

 **Let's Sing**

Two Little Snails

(Tune: "Three Little Ducks Went Out to Play," or chant)

Two little snails,
(make two fists [shells], with thumbs sticking out [heads])

Moving to and fro,
(wiggle thumbs [heads])

Slithered through my garden,
Wouldn't you know.
(hands out, palms up)

When they saw a tomato,
(hand shading eyes as you look)

Nice and ripe,
(rub tummy)

They took a nibble,
(take bites alternately with hands)

Bite, bite, …
YIPE!
(throw both hands up in the air)

Repeat using different fruits and vegetables.

 **Let's Play**

Snail Shell Relay

The setup: Cut the bottom out of a paper grocery bag to make a snail's shell. Adjust the length and make the ends smooth by folding the ends under and taping. Set two carpet squares several feet apart. Line up evenly behind the carpet squares.

The game: The first person in one of the lines puts on the snail's shell, holding it up around his middle, and races to the other carpet square. Then he removes the shell and gives it to the first person in that line, who races back. Play continues until everyone has had a turn.

Slithering Snake

 Let's Sing

Slither, Slide, and Hiss
(Chant)

Can a s-s-s-snake, s-s-s-snake, s-s-s-snake,
S-s-s-slither, s-s-s-slither, s-s-s-slither?
> *(make a snake's head by touching your thumb to your fingers;
> slither and slide your hand over your arm, head, face, etc.)*

Can a s-s-s-snake, s-s-s-snake, s-s-s-snake,
S-s-s-slide, s-s-s-slide, s-s-s-slide?
> *(slide as you do the actions described above)*

Can a s-s-s-snake, s-s-s-snake, s-s-s-snake,
Hiss-s-s-s, hiss-s-s-s, hiss-s-s-s?
> *(hiss as you do the actions described above)*

The ans-s-swer is-s-s-s,
Yes-s-s-s, yes-s-s-s, yes-s-s-s!
> *(nod your snake head yes, yes, yes)*

NATURE NOTES
Hiss-s-s-s-s-s!

Snakes in a garden are usually a good thing. Garden snakes eat insects and
small animals like mice or moles that may want to munch in your garden. All
snakes, large and small, are *predators*, which means that they eat other animals.

No matter how big their meal, snakes do not chew their food. They swallow
their food whole! Some snakes can unhook their jaws so that their mouth can
stretch wide open. Imagine that!

Look for the simple shapes in a snake. Can you see the "S" shape?

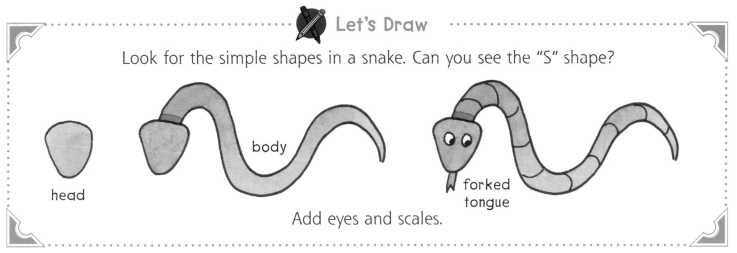

head

body

forked tongue

Add eyes and scales.

Let's Play

Slithering Snakes Relay

Snakes don't have arms or legs. But they do have flexible spines and strong muscles that help them as they slither across the ground. Can you slither across the ground without using your arms or legs?

The setup: Create a tunnel with sheets, blankets, and chairs. Players line up in even groups at opposite ends of the tunnel. Choose one person to be the first Snake.

The game: The Snake gets down on her tummy and slithers through the tunnel. (Don't forget to hiss!) When she reaches the other end, the first person in that line becomes the new Snake and slithers through the tunnel. Play continues until everyone has had a turn to be the Snake.

Sssss

LITTLE HANDS
Story Corner™

❋❋❋❋❋❋❋❋❋❋❋❋

Verdi by Janell Cannon

A Snake Mistake
by Mavis Smith

Snakes
by Patricia Demuth

Snakes
by Deborah Dennard

Snake Sock Puppet

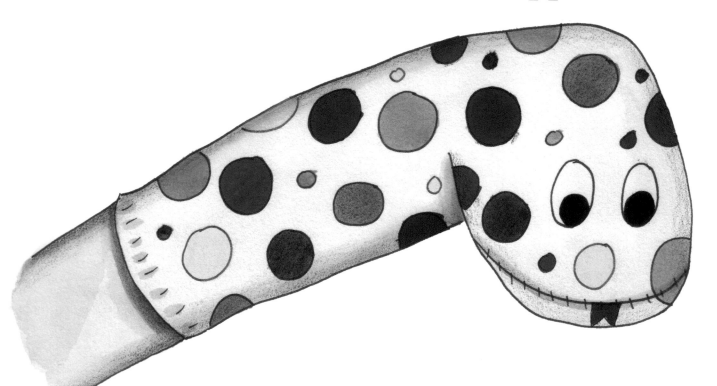

SSSSS

SSSSS

WHAT YOU NEED

⟳ White sock
⟳ Piece of cardboard
⟳ Markers

WHAT YOU DO

1. Stick a long piece of cardboard into the sock. Use markers to color your sock snake. Let your snake dry before removing the cardboard.

2. Put the sock on your hand and watch your slithery snake come to life. Repeat "SLITHER, SLIDE, AND HISS" on page 62.

At the Zoo

Going to the zoo is fun to do,
Come along with me and you'll see it's true.

Watch the elephants, monkeys, and bears,
Create a hippo, or a lion in its lair.

Strut like a peacock, be a giraffe reaching tall,
Roar like the animals — can you hear their calls?

Sing and dance, do the kangaroo hop,
The zoo is so exciting, you won't want to stop!

See the Elephants!

Start your trip to the zoo with the elephants. They are so amazing, with their long, powerful trunks, and they're so much fun to watch with their huge, wiggly ears!

 Let's Sing

The Elephants' Twist

(Tune: "We're Going to the Zoo," or chant)

Elephants twist, twist, twist,
(stand in a circle and twist)
Just like this, this, this.
Elephants twist, twist, twist,
Just like this, this, this.

Elephants swing, swing, swing,
(clasp your hands, hold arms in front of you, and swing them side-to-side like a trunk)
Just doing their thing, thing, thing.
Elephants swing, swing, swing,
Just doing their thing, thing, thing.

More verses:

Elephants dance, dance, dance,
(dance)
They take a chance, chance, chance …

Elephants run, run, run,
(run in a circle)
Having fun, fun, fun …

Elephants skip, skip, skip,
(skip in a circle)
Just don't trip, trip, trip …

Elephants play, play, play,
(raise hands up and turn in a circle)
In the hay, hay, hay …

Elephants stretch, stretch, stretch,
(stretch arms alternately over head)
Playing catch, catch, catch …

Elephants sleep, sleep, sleep,
(sing quietly, resting head on hands)
Not a peep, peep, peep …

NATURE NOTES

Traveling trunks!

An elephant's nose is called a *trunk*. Elephants use their trunks for breathing, smelling, picking things up, drinking, and bathing. An elephant can use its trunk to pick up things as small and delicate as a peanut or as big and heavy as a tree!

 Let's Play

Trunk Push Relay

The setup: An equal number of players line up behind two carpet squares placed 15 to 20 feet (5 to 7 m) apart. Place an upside-down bucket or laundry basket in front of the first person in the starting line.

The game: At the signal, the starting player creates an elephant's trunk by clasping his hands together, and then uses his trunk to push the bucket from one carpet square to the next. When he reaches the other side, the first person in that line becomes the Elephant. Play continues until everyone has had a turn.

 Let's Draw

Look for the simple shapes in this clever elephant.

head

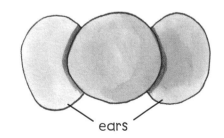

ears

legs

trunk

Try drawing the trunk in different positions. Draw lines coming out of the trunk to make the elephant look as if it is spraying water.
Is it spraying itself or is it spraying another elephant?

 Let's Create

Elephant Mask

WHAT YOU NEED

- Sponge
- Gray tempera paint, in a jar lid
- Large paper plate
- Child-safety scissors
- Gray or light blue construction paper
- Stapler
- Tape
- Craft or Popsicle stick

EARS

TRUNK

step 2

WHAT YOU DO

1. Dip a sponge in gray paint and dab it onto the paper plate. Let it dry.

2. Cut the elephant's ears and trunk from construction paper. Staple them to the paper plate. Have a grown-up help you curl the elephant's trunk.

3. Cut two eyeholes in the mask.

4. Tape a craft or Popsicle stick to the back of the mask.

LITTLE HANDS
Story Corner™

Miss Mary Mack by Mary Ann Hoberman

Elmer by David McKee

1, 2, 3 to the Zoo by Eric Carle

The Saggy Baggy Elephant by K. and B. Jackson

Roaring Lion

A lion's family is called a *pride*,
They work and play side by side.

 Let's Sing

One Little Lion at the Zoo

(Tune: "One Little Duck Went Out to Play," or chant)

One little lion at the zoo,
  (tuck thumb in fist)

One little lion plays peek-a-boo!
  (pop thumb out)

One little lion out of sight,
  (tuck thumb in fist)

One little lion roars with all its might!
  (pop thumb out and ROAR!)

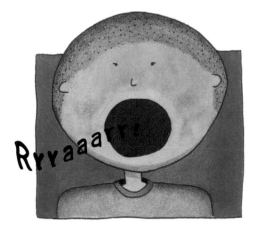

Rrraaarr!

More verses:
Repeat the fingerplays for the first three verses and change the last verse's fingerplay according to the type of animal.

One tall giraffe at the zoo,
One tall giraffe plays peek-a-boo!
One tall giraffe, out of sight,
One tall giraffe strrrr-et-ches with all its might!
  (stretch thumb up)

One big elephant at the zoo,
One big elephant plays peek-a-boo!
One big elephant out of sight,
One big elephant trumpets with all its might!
  (make elephant trumpeting sound)

Now, have fun and make up more of your own verses with fingerplays! Here are a few to get you started:

Springy kangaroo ... hops
  (fingers of one hand "hop" off other arm)

Pretty peacock ... struts
  (open hand, shake fingers)

NATURE NOTES

Me-ow! G-rrr! Ro-ar!

Do you have a cat? If you do, then you know that house cats can be great pets — gentle, cuddly, and fun to play with. But do you know there are other kinds of cats that aren't kept as pets? There is a *lynx*, a *jaguar*, and a *bobcat*, to name a few. Can you think of any more? Here's a hint: You might see this big cat at a circus or in a zoo. It may have a fluffy mane around its face? Now, can you guess what this cat is called?

Lion Lacing

WHAT YOU NEED

- Large paper plate
- Yellow tempera paint, in a jar lid
- Paintbrush
- Pencil
- Tape
- Yarn, 5 1/2 feet (165 cm) long, any colors
- Black marker

LITTLE HANDS
Story Corner™

How Loud Is a Lion? by Clare Beaton
Big Red Tub by Julia Jarman
Our Cat Cuddles by Gervase Phinn

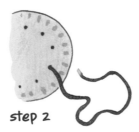

step 2

WHAT YOU DO

1. Paint the paper plate yellow. Let it dry. Have a grown-up help you use a pencil to carefully poke holes around the center of the plate.

2. Wrap a piece of tape around one end of the yarn to create a dull needle. Tie the other end of the yarn to the plate. Lace the yarn through the holes and around the outside of the plate to create a mane.

3. Use the marker to draw the lion's face.

Note: You can change yarn colors or add more yarn by tying off the yarn ends at the holes, or taping yarn ends to the back of the plate. Make the mane as thick or thin as you'd like. You can lace around the center holes to outline the face.

Let's Play

The Lion Pokey

(Tune: "Hokey Pokey," or chant)

You put your claws in,
(stand in circle, put hands in to center with fingers spread)

You put your claws out,
(put hands out of circle)

You put your claws in,
And you shake them all about.
(put hands into center and shake them)

You do the Lion Pokey
(hands over head)

And you turn yourself around.
(turn in circle)

That's what it's all about!
(clap hands, ROAR!)

NATURE NOTES

A kingly beast.

A lion's *mane* (the ring of bushy hair around the head, neck, and shoulders of a boy, or male, lion) can grow up to 20 inches (50 cm) long. Adult male lions are the only types of cats that have a mane. Do you think the mane makes the lion look more ferocious to other animals?

Let's Draw

Look for the simple shapes in a lion.

head

body

legs

Add a line to separate its legs. Add eyes and a tail. Draw a mane.
Make your lion look like the "king of the jungle" by drawing a crown on top of its head.

Tall, Tall Giraffe

 Let's Create

Towering Giraffe Puppet

WHAT YOU NEED

- ◉ 3 large paper plates
- ◉ Child-safety scissors
- ◉ Black marker
- ◉ Yellow and brown tempera paint, in separate jar lids
- ◉ Paintbrush
- ◉ Brown and orange construction paper
- ◉ Stapler

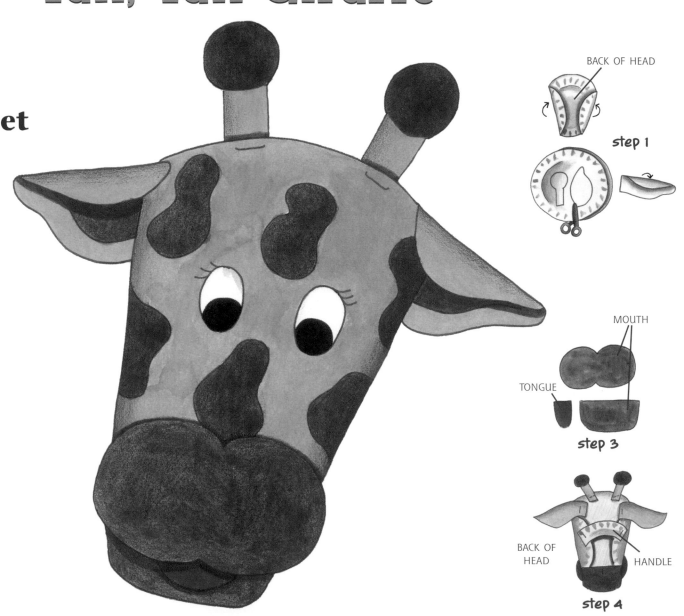

BACK OF HEAD

step 1

MOUTH

TONGUE

step 3

BACK OF HEAD

HANDLE

step 4

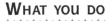

WHAT YOU DO

1. Fold in two sides of one paper plate to create the giraffe's long head. Place the other two paper plates on top of each other. Cut out the ears and horns. Fold the side of each ear forward.

2. Use a black marker to draw eyes on the face. Paint the giraffe yellow with brown spots.

3. Cut the tongue and mouth pieces from construction paper. Staple them to the face.

4. Staple a scrap from the paper plate's rim to the back of the giraffe's head to use as a handle.

5. Sing "THE GIRAFFE AND THE TALL, TALL TREE" (page 74) while holding your giraffe puppet way up high!

LITTLE HANDS Story Corner™

Never Too Little to Love by Jeanne Willis
A Giraffe and a Half by Shel Silverstein

 Let's Sing

The Acacia Tree

(Tune: "Here We Go 'Round the Mulberry Bush," or chant)

A giraffe's favorite food is
acacia (uh-KAY-shuh) tree leaves.

Here we go 'round the acacia tree,
(walk in a circle holding arms or giraffe puppet above your head)

The acacia tree, the acacia tree.
Here we go 'round the acacia tree,
When we're at the zoo.

**More action verses to
play in the circle:**

This is the way we stretch our necks
(stop and stretch way up high)

Reach down low
(spread legs, reach down low)

Swish our tails
(wiggle rear end)

Stick out our tongues
(stick your tongue out as far as you can)

Run away
(run in a circle, arms above your head)

 Let's Sing

The Giraffe and the Tall, Tall Tree

(Tune: "Apple Tree," or chant)

Way up high in the tall, tall tree
(reach both hands above head, wiggle fingers)

Three little leaves looked down at me.
(hold up three fingers)

I stretched my neck as far as I could,
(stretch arms above head, hold hands like a giraffe's head)

I stretched out my tongue,
(stick tongue out really far)

Slurp,
(slurp tongue in)

Mmmm, they were good!
(rub tummy)

NATURE NOTES

World's tallest animal!

Everything about a giraffe is long: its legs, its body, its tail, its neck, and even its tongue! In fact, the giraffe is the world's tallest animal, towering above all the others. That makes it easy to reach leaves way up high in the trees. With its height and good eyesight, a giraffe can also see trouble coming from far away and use its long legs to take very long *strides*, or steps, and get away!

Let's Draw

The spots on a giraffe are like fingerprints — no two are alike! Look for the simple shapes in this giraffe.

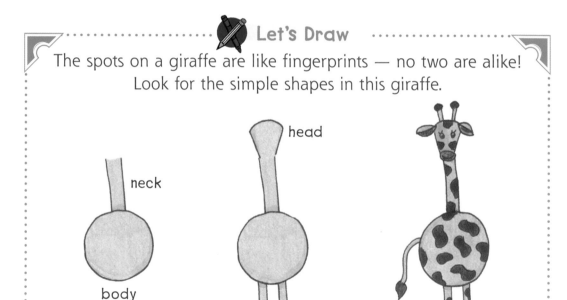

Add spots and a tail. Draw trees with leaves for your giraffe to eat.

Huge Hippo

 Let's Sing

Hungry, Hungry Hippo

(Tune: "I'm a Little Teapot," or chant)

Hungry, hungry hippo,
(hold arms in circle out front, rock side to side)

Oh-h-h, so-o-o sl-o-o-w—
(take a giant, exaggerated, slow-motion step forward)

Walk into the water,
(slap hands alternately in rhythm like steps)

And down ... you ... go!
(raise hands over head, squat down, slap ground)

 Let's Play

Hippo Hop

The setup: Place carpet squares or pillows in a line, representing the backs of hippos in an alligator swamp.

The game: Make your way across the jungle swamp by hopping across on the backs of the hippos. Don't fall in or an alligator might eat you!

Happy Hippopotamus

WHAT YOU NEED

- 🌀 Child-safety scissors
- 🌀 3 large paper plates
- 🌀 Stapler
- 🌀 Gray and pink tempera paint, in separate jar lids
- 🌀 Paintbrush
- 🌀 Paper plate scraps or scrap paper
- 🌀 Black marker
- 🌀 Tape
- 🌀 Newspaper

step 1

step 2

step 3

step 4

WHAT YOU DO

1. Cut one paper plate in half. Fold the second paper plate in half. Staple each half plate to the back of the folded plate to create two pockets.

2. Paint the outside of both pockets gray. Let them dry. Flip the plate over. Create the hippo's mouth by painting the center of the plate pink. Paint the rim of the plate gray. Let paint dry.

3. Fold the third plate in half, then open it. Cut the bottom half of the plate into a point. Cut off the tip. Tuck it into the front pocket. Staple the plate in place (to the top pocket only) to create the hippo's forehead.

4. Cut the ears, eyes, nostrils, and teeth from paper scraps. Use a black marker to draw eyeballs and nostrils.

5. Staple the ears to the top of the forehead. Paint the nostrils, forehead, and ears gray. Let paint dry. Use tape to attach the eyes, nostrils, and teeth.

6. Wad up small pieces of newspaper and stuff the mouth pockets from the back of the head.

NATURE NOTES

Rock-a-bye Baby Hippo!

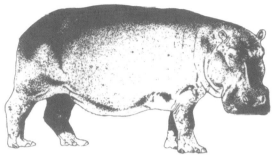

If you think hippos weigh a lot, then you are absolutely correct! In fact, when a hippo is born, it already weighs between 50 to 90 pounds (22.5 to 40.5 kg). That's about as much as some third- to seventh-graders weigh in school. Do you know how much you weighed when you were born?

Hippos have very short, sturdy legs to carry all of that weight. Look at the picture above, and then decide: Are your legs longer than a hippo's? Are they wider than a hippo's? How would a bird's legs compare to a hippo's?

LITTLE HANDS Story Corner™

Hippos Go Berserk by Sandra Boynton

Kiss, Kiss! by Margaret Wild

The Hippo-Not-Amus by Tony and Jan Payne

NATURE NOTES

Wrinkly skin?

What do you notice about your skin when you play in your bathtub for a long time? Are your fingers all wrinkled up like a raisin? Well, guess what? A hippopotamus stays in the water for as long as 18 hours each day! That's longer than the time from when you get up in the morning until you go to bed at night. The water helps the hippo stay cool and keep its skin moist by protecting it from the hot African sun.

 ## Let's Draw

Look at the simple shapes in a hippopotamus. Notice how its eyes, ears, and nostrils are on the top of its head. Now, compare the *hippo's* features with where your eyes, ears, and nose are on *your* head. What is the difference?

The different position on a hippo makes it possible for the hippo to hear, see, and breathe at the surface of the water, while the rest of its body is safely hidden underwater.

Try drawing the side view of a hippopotamus. Use a wide oval beside the hippo's head for its body. Add four legs and a short tail.

Monkey Business

Short or long, without fail,
A monkey always has a tail.

 Let's Sing

Five Little Monkeys

(Traditional rhyme or chant)

Five little monkeys jumping on the bed,
(bounce five fingers up and down on palm)

One fell off and bumped its head.
(bounce one finger to the floor, rub head)

Momma called the doctor and the doctor said,
(pretend to call on the phone)

"No more monkeys jumping on the bed!"
(wag finger back and forth)

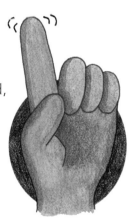

**Repeat with four monkeys, then three,
then two monkeys, then one.**

No little monkeys jumping on the bed,
(hold hands out to side, palms up)

None fell off and bumped their heads.
(hit floor, rub head)

Momma called the doctor and the doctor said,
(pretend to call on the phone)

"Get those monkeys back on the bed!"
(wag finger back and forth)

Variation: Jump up and down (line 1), squat to the ground (line 2), pretend to call on the phone (line 3), wag finger back and forth (line 4).

NATURE NOTES

Many monkeys.

No visit to the zoo is complete without a trip to see the monkeys! They are so much fun to watch swinging from the tree limbs and chattering away.

There are many different kinds of monkeys in the wild. The *marmoset* monkey is the smallest, about the size of a small squirrel, and the *mandrill* is the largest. All monkeys have tails. Some tails are long, and some tails are very short. Some tails are called *prehensile* tails, which means that they can grasp onto tree branches, just like you can grasp something using your thumb and fingers.

LITTLE HANDS Story Corner™

Five Little Monkeys Jumping On the Bed by Eileen Christelow

Naughty Little Monkeys by Jim Aylesworth

One Monkey Too Many by Jackie French Koller

Caps for Sale by Esphyr Slobodkina

Monkeys by Deborah Dennard

Let's Create

Jumping Monkey Straw Puppets

WHAT YOU NEED

- Pencil and paper or photocopy of MONKEY template
- Child-safety scissors
- Construction paper
- Markers
- Tape
- 3 clear plastic drinking straws
- Sturdy paper cup

WHAT YOU DO

1. Use a pencil and tracing paper (or a photocopier) to copy the MONKEY template (page 81). Cut out the copied pattern.

2. Trace the pattern onto the construction paper with a pencil to make three monkeys. Cut out the monkeys. Use markers to color the eyes and add details.

3. Tape one monkey onto the end of each of the three straws. Ask a grown-up to punch three holes in the bottom of a sturdy paper cup. Turn the cup upside down. Put one straw in each hole.

4. Repeat the "FIVE LITTLE MONKEYS" rhyme (page 79), using "three" instead of "five." Make the monkeys jump up and down by holding the bottom of the straws and pushing them up and down. Each time a monkey falls off the bed, remove a straw from your cup.

MONKEY TEMPLATE

Trace or photocopy the MONKEY template onto a piece of paper to make your own pattern. *(Please do not cut this template out of this book. Thank you.)*

Let's Play

Banana Relay

The setup: Players line up behind two carpet squares placed 15 to 20 feet (5 to 7 m) apart. Give the first person in the starting line a banana (paper, plastic, or a real one) to hold.

The game: At the signal, the player holding the banana races from one square to the other, handing off the banana to the next Monkey in line. Play continues until everyone has had a turn.

Big Bear

 Let's Sing

Brown Bear, Brown Bear

(Tune: "Teddy Bear, Teddy Bear," or chant)

Brown bear, Brown bear,
(make a big circle with arms out front)

In his cave so deep.
(raise circle over head)

Brown bear, Brown bear,
(lower circle out front)

Snoring loudly, fast asleep.
(rest head on hands, pretend snore)

Brown bear, Brown bear,
(make a big circle with arms out front)

Wakes up with a scowl.
(place hands on hips, scowl)

Brown bear, Brown bear,
(make a big circle with arms out front)

Wakes up with a growl!
(growl loudly!)

Grrr!
Grrr!
Grrr!

 Let's Play

Bear's Cave

Many bears that live in cold parts of the world spend their winters in caves or dens. They make a cozy nest where they can sleep without eating or drinking for as long as six months. This long winter sleep is called *hibernation*.

Pretend you are a bear and hibernate. Use a tent or blankets draped over chairs to create a bear's cave. Crawl into the cave on all fours and then come out growling like a bear!

 Let's Create

Big Bear

WHAT YOU NEED

- Child-safety scissors
- Brown paper grocery bag
- Sponge
- Brown tempera paint, in a jar lid
- Black marker

step 1

step 2

WHAT YOU DO

1. Cut along the seam of a large paper grocery bag to open it up. Cut the bottom panel off.

2. Draw a large bear onto the grocery bag. Cut it out. (If you fold the bag into thirds, you can get three large bears per bag.)

3. Dip a sponge into brown paint and dab it onto the bear. Use a black marker to draw eyes, ears, a nose, and a mouth.

More Fun: Partially staple two bear shapes together. Stuff the bear with newspaper and staple it closed, for a big bear you can hug!

NATURE NOTES

Bear hugs.

When you wrap your arms around someone and give them a great big hug, it's called a bear hug. Bears don't really hug each other, so why do we call hugs, bear hugs? It might be because when bears fight they stand on their hind legs and wrap their arms around each other. From a distance it looks as if they are giving each other a big hug.

Give someone you love a big bear hug!

LITTLE HANDS Story Corner™

Brown Bear, Brown Bear, What Do You See?
by Bill Martin Jr.

We're Going on a Bear Hunt
by Michael Rosen and Helen Oxenbury

The Bear: An American Folk Song
by Kenneth J. Spengler

 Let's Draw

A baby bear is called a *cub*. A mommy (female) bear is called a *sow*.
A daddy (male) bear is called a *boar*. That makes three bears! Do you know the fairy tale about the three bears? Now, can you make up a story to tell about a real bear?

head

body

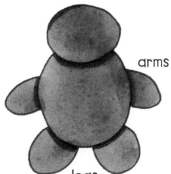
arms
legs

Look at the simple shapes in these bears. Can you draw a bear family?

Jumping Kangaroo

 Let's Play

Kangaroo Jump

Standing Long Jump

Ask a grown-up to help you. Place a piece of tape on the floor. Stand behind the line and jump as far as you can. Put a piece of tape on the floor to mark your landing spot. Try it two or three times to find your best jump. What did you do to make your best jump?

Running Long Jump

Ask a grown-up to help you. Place a piece of tape on the floor. Stand 10 to 15 feet (3 to 5 m) behind the line. Run until you reach the tape, then jump as far as you can (be sure you have something soft to land on, like some pillows or an exercise mat!). Put a piece of tape on the floor where you landed. Try it two or three times to find your best jump.

Let's Sing

Kangaroo Hop

(Tune: "Skip to My Lou," or chant)

Hop, hop, kangaroo hop,
  (jump up and down)

Hop, hop, kangaroo hop,

Hop, hop, kangaroo hop.

Hop, hop, hop, until you drop!
  (drop to the ground)

NATURE NOTES

Long jumpers.

There are almost 60 different kinds of kangaroos. The smallest kangaroo is the *musky rat* kangaroo. It is as small as a rat! The largest kangaroo is the *red* kangaroo. It is the size of a person, or bigger!

Kangaroos are good jumpers. Large kangaroos can easily jump 29 feet (about 10 m) in a single hop. A *gray* kangaroo once made a single jump longer than a school bus! Play KANGAROO JUMP to see how far you can hop!

 Let's Create

Momma and Baby Kangaroo

Kangaroos are a type of animal known as a *marsupial*. Marsupials carry their young in special body pockets called *pouches*. When a baby kangaroo (called a *joey*) is born, it is very tiny and can't see or hear. It doesn't even have hair!

Five or six months later, when the joey finally emerges from the mother kangaroo's pouch, it looks totally different. It has hair, it can see and hear, and it is ready to start hopping around and exploring the world. Have fun making your own momma kangaroo with her joey!

POUCH

FOLD BACK
AND STAPLE

step 1

HEAD

FOOT

TAIL

step 2

WHAT YOU NEED

- Child-safety scissors
- 5 large paper plates
- Stapler
- Pencil
- Construction paper
- KANGAROO BABY (JOEY) template (optional)
- Sponge or paintbrush
- Brown tempera paint, in a jar lid
- Black marker

WHAT YOU DO

1. To create the kangaroo's pouch, cut the top off of one paper plate. Staple the pouch to the second paper plate. Fold the edges of both plates back. Staple.

2. Cut the kangaroo's head from the third paper plate, and the tail and foot from the fourth paper plate. Staple them to the body.

3. Cut the ears from the fifth paper plate. Cut a slit in each ear. Overlap the bottom of each ear, then staple to the kangaroo's head.

4. Draw a baby kangaroo on construction paper, or trace and use the KANGAROO BABY (JOEY) template if you want. Cut it out.

5. Paint your kangaroos. Use a black marker to add eyes and noses. Then place the baby kangaroo in its mother's pouch!

KANGAROO BABY (JOEY) TEMPLATE

Trace or photocopy the KANGAROO BABY (JOEY) template onto a piece of paper to make your own pattern. *(Please do not cut this template out of this book. Thank you.)*

LITTLE HANDS Story Corner™

McGillycuddy Could! by Pamela Duncan Edwards

Does a Kangaroo Have a Mother, Too? by Eric Carle

Marsupial Sue by John Lithgow

Who Are You, Baby Kangaroo? by Stella Blackstone and Clare Beaton

Zoobooks Kangaroos by Beth Wagner Brust

Proud Peacock

 **Let's Create**

Peacock Stick Puppet

WHAT YOU NEED

- Child-safety scissors
- Construction paper (assorted colors)
- Glue
- Black marker
- Large paper plate
- Colorful craft feathers
- Assorted sequins, pom-poms, and other decorations
- Tape
- Craft or Popsicle stick

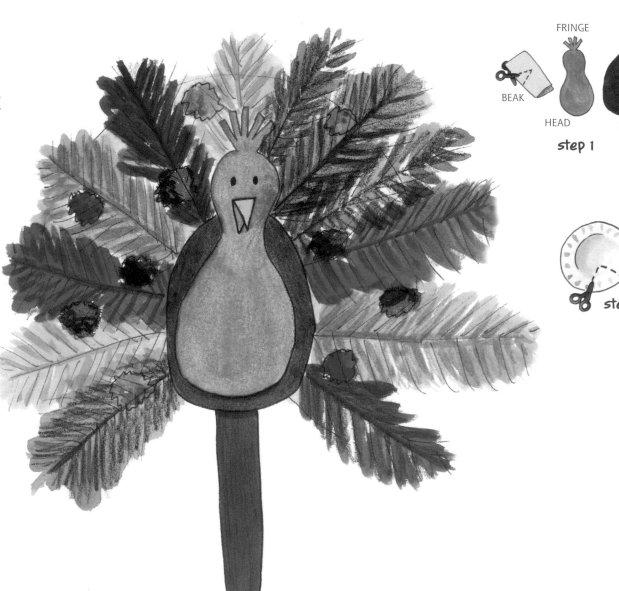

FRINGE

BEAK

HEAD

BODY

step 1

step 3

WHAT YOU DO

1. Cut a peacock head from construction paper. Create crest feathers by cutting a triangle of fringe on top of the head. Cut a peacock body from construction paper. To create a beak, fold a small piece of paper in half and cut out a triangle.

2. Glue the head to the body and the beak onto the head. Use a marker to draw eyes.

3. Cut a wedge from the paper plate. This is where you will put the body of the peacock. Glue feathers onto the plate. Glue sequins, pom-poms, and other decorations on top of the feathers.

4. Glue the body onto the feathered plate. Tape a craft stick to the back of the plate. Color the stick with markers, if desired.

Let's Play
Peacock Feather Relay

The setup: Make a large construction-paper peacock head to hang on the wall. Line up 10 to 15 feet (3 to 5 m) away. Each player gets a craft feather, or a feather cut from construction paper, with tape attached to the back.

The game: The first person in line runs his feather to the peacock and attaches it. Then he runs back and the next person in line goes. Continue until everyone has hung a feather on the peacock.

 Let's Sing

Pretty Peacock

(Tune: "The Grand Old Duke of York," or chant)

There was a pretty peacock,
(hold thumb in front of four fingers)

Who lived in the zoo.

It had so many feathers,
(wiggle four fingers)

It didn't know what to do.
(hold hands out to side, palms up)

It shook them to the left,
(shake fingers to the left)

It shook them to the right.
(shake fingers to the right)

It shook them and it shook them,
(shake fingers in front)

Right out of sight!
(put both hands behind back)

NATURE NOTES

Pretty as a peacock.

The male (boy) peacock has beautiful, long, blue and green feathers that trail behind it in a train. When it tries to attract attention, it lifts its train and spreads the tail feathers in a fan that arches over its back. The girl (female) peafowl is called a *peahen.* Her colors, as in many of nature's females, are less colorful and she does not have a train of feathers. Can you think of any other kinds of birds that have brightly colored males and less colorful females? What about ducks? Or robins?

LITTLE HANDS Story Corner™

Dr. Seuss's Gertrude McFuzz by Dr. Seuss

My School's a Zoo! by Stu Smith

At the Zoo by Judy Press

On the Farm

On the farm where the animals play,
It's lots of fun to spend the day.

Make a goat or maybe some sheep,
Pretend you're a chick, "Cheep, cheep, cheep."

"Run" with the horses or "feed" the pigs,
You're sure to have fun that's big, BIG, BIG!

On the farm where the animals play,
That's where I want to spend my day!

Barn Boogie

Barns are built for many different uses. Some barns are built to house and care for animals. Other barns are built to store food and equipment. Imagine what it would be like to live in a barn. Do you think it would be comfortable sleeping in hay? Lie down in some soft grass to give it a try!

 Let's Sing

Go In and Out the Barn Door

(Tune: "Go In and Out the Window," or chant)

Go in and out the barn door.
(hold hands in a circle, walk in and out of the center)

Go in and out the barn door.

Go in and out the barn door,

As we have done before.

Go in and be a horse.
(walk to center slapping legs and neigh)

Go out and be a horse.
(walk out slapping legs and neigh)

Go in and be a horse.
(walk to center slapping legs and neigh)

As we have done before.
(walk out slapping legs and neigh)

Additional Verses: Cow *(make horns with fingers and moo)*, Rooster *(flap wings and crow)*, Pig *(flatten nose and oink)*, and so on.

NATURE NOTES

From the Farm to You!

Visit your local Farmer's Market to see what kinds of fruits and vegetables are grown where you live. Ask the farmers how long it takes to grow their fruits and vegetables, or if they have animals on their farm. If there isn't a Farmer's Market nearby, talk to the people at the *produce* (fresh fruits and vegetables) department at a grocery store. Find out where your fruits and vegetables come from, and how long they last once they get to the store.

 Let's Play

Animals-in-the-Barn Charades

The setup: Using a tent, or blankets draped over furniture or a clothesline, make a "barn." Choose one person to be the Actor. Everyone else will be the audience, sitting near the barn.

The game: The Actor walks into the barn. When she comes out of the barn, she pretends to be a farm animal, using actions but *without making any sounds*. The audience guesses what animal the Actor is pretending to be. The player who guesses correctly becomes the next Actor.

Actor Strategy:
◆ Think about how the animal moves. Does it walk on two legs or four? Can it fly? Is it fast or slow?

◆ Think about how the animal looks. Use your hands and arms to create body parts like feathers, horns, beaks, tails, etc.

◆ Think about how the animal looks as it makes a sound. Does it stretch its neck up high? Does it flap its wings? Don't make the sound, but you can act as if you are!

Audience Strategy:
◆ Watch the Actor carefully for clues about how the animal moves, acts, and looks.

◆ Try to remember all of the different clues as the Actor gives them to you, because he may not be able to act out all of the clues at the same time.

✋ Let's Create

Big Red Barn

WHAT YOU NEED

- 2 paper plates
- Child-safety scissors
- Yellow crayon
- Paint, in a jar lid
- Paintbrush or sponge
- Yarn
- Stapler
- Farm animal stickers or markers

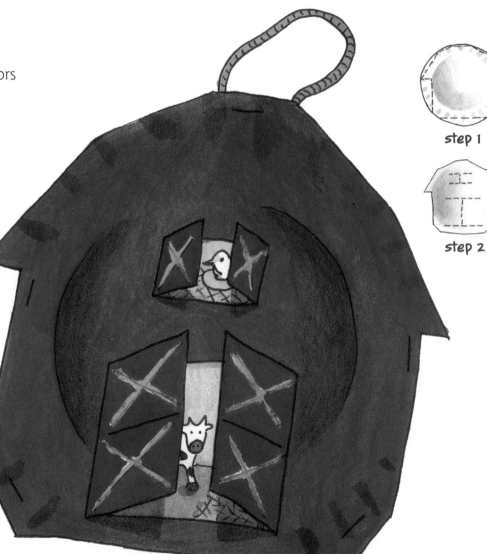

step 1

step 2

WHAT YOU DO

1. Place the two paper plates together and cut them into a barn shape.

2. Ask a grown-up to help cut open the barn doors in the top paper plate.

3. Draw details on the doors with a yellow crayon. Paint the barn; let dry.

4. Make a loop with yarn. Place it between the barn pieces, at the top, and staple it in place. Staple the top and bottom pieces together on the sides.

5. Decorate the barn with farm animal stickers or draw your own farm animals.

Cock-a-Doodle-Do!

Arooster begins his day at sunrise by singing a very loud crowing song. While the rooster's song makes a good alarm clock for everyone on the farm, the crowing actually marks his territory and warns other roosters to stay away. And why do we refer to all roosters as "he"? That's because all roosters are males, or boys.

Can you crow like a rooster?

 Let's Sing

All Around the Farmyard

(Tune: "Pop Goes the Weasel," or chant)

All around the farmyard,
(hold hands and walk in a circle)

The animals were sleeping.
The rooster thought 'twas time to wake up,
Sh-h-h-h,
(stop and squat down, put finger to lips)

1-2-3,
(hold up fingers)

R-r-r-r-rrrrrrrr!
(tuck arms and flap wings as you crow like a rooster)

Up jumped the animals!
(jump up high!)

LITTLE HANDS
Story Corner™

Snappy Little Farmyard: Spend a Day on Snappy Farm by Dugald Steer

Elvis the Rooster Almost Goes to Heaven by Denys Cazet

Baby Einstein: Baby MacDonald on the Farm by Julie Aigner-Clark

 Let's Play

Farmyard Fun

Hold onto the edges of a parachute, blanket, or towel. Place beach balls or small stuffed animals in the center of the parachute.

Walk in a circle as you sing "ALL AROUND THE FARMYARD" (page 95). After the rooster crows, pop the parachute or blanket way up high so that all of the animals fly off the parachute!

NATURE NOTES

What's that sound?

There are a lot of sounds on a farm or in the city, and they change all the time. Sit outside and listen. What kinds of sounds do you hear? Maybe there are birds chirping, or cars going by. Try listening in the early morning, in the afternoon, and again in the evening. Do you hear the same sounds or are they different? When are sounds the loudest? When are they quietest?

LITTLE HANDS
Story Corner™

Big Red Barn by Margaret Wise Brown

Skip to My Lou by Mary Ann Hoberman and Nadine Bernard Westcott

The Napping House by Audrey Wood

 **Let's Draw**

Look for the simple shapes in a rooster.

 head

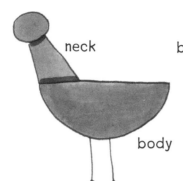 neck

body

 beak

tail

legs

Now you try! When drawing a rooster's head (or something else), it doesn't need to look the same as what you see in a book. Experiment by facing your rooster in other directions. Or, try making a rooster in different poses. For a rooster that looks like he is eating, attach his head to the front of his chest with his beak facing the ground.

NATURE NOTES

A real farm!

Visit a farm, if you can, to touch, see, smell, and hear the life on the farm. If there isn't a farm nearby, watch a farm video or DVD. Try to imagine what the farm would smell like. Can you think of pleasant smells and unpleasant smells? Do you think all of the animals would have soft fur? Which animal would make the loudest sounds? Which ones would be the "quietest?" Which animal would you be most excited to see?

 **Let's Create**

Rooster Stick Puppet

A rooster has a *beak* instead of a nose and mouth, a *wattle* that hangs at his neck, and a *comb* that sits on top of his head. Look in the mirror and imagine what you would look like with a beak, a wattle, and a comb!

WHAT YOU NEED

- Pencil
- Tracing paper (or photocopy)
- Child-safety scissors
- Tape
- 3 paper plates (2¹/₂ per puppet)
- Markers
- Stapler
- Craft or Popsicle stick
- Glue
- Feathers (optional)

step 2

trim

step 3

step 4

WHAT YOU DO

1. Draw your own rooster's head (page 97), or using a pencil and tracing paper (or a photocopier) copy the ROOSTER'S HEAD template. Cut out the copied pattern.

2. Tape the rooster pattern to the back of one paper plate and trace around the pattern with a pencil. Cut out the paper-plate head, with its beak, wattle, and comb. Use markers to color the rooster's face.

3. Fold the second plate in half. Cut a slit on the fold long enough for your rooster's head to slide in. Staple the head in place; trim. Cut another slit on the fold from the other end for the rooster's tail.

4. Cut the third plate in half, using a half-plate for the rooster's tail. Slide the tail into the slit. Staple in place.

5. Tape a craft or Popsicle stick to the inside of the folded plate. Staple the plate shut on each side of the stick.

6. Spread glue onto the rooster. Add feathers.

ROOSTER'S HEAD TEMPLATE

Trace or photocopy the ROOSTER'S HEAD template onto a piece of paper to make your own pattern. (Please do not cut this template out of this book. Thank you.)

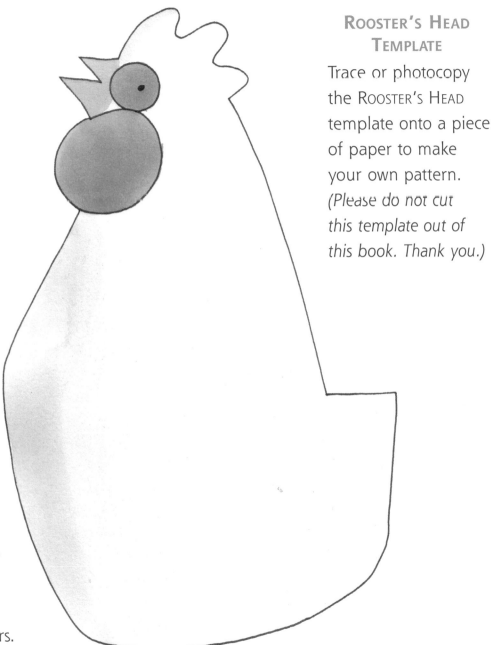

The Hen House

A hen has a beak, a wattle, and a comb just as a rooster does.
And just as all roosters are boys, all hens are females, or girls.

Pretend you are a hen. Instead of two hands, you have wings.
Instead of a mouth with teeth, you have a beak. How would you eat your
favorite foods or play your favorite games? Peck, peck, peck, like a hen!

LITTLE HANDS
Story Corner™

Daisy Comes Home
by Jan Brett

The Little Red Hen
by Lucinda McQueen

Miss Hunnicutt's Hat
by Jeff Brumbeau

*I Love You! A Bushel and a
Peck* by Frank Loesser

Here a Chick, Where a Chick?
by Suse MacDonald

Let's Sing

Mother Hen

(Tune: "Twinkle, Twinkle Little Star," or chant)

Mother, mother, mother hen,
(tuck arms and flap wings)

Sitting on those eggs, all ten.
(cup hands; hold up ten fingers)

With a snap and a crackle, and a pop, pop, pop.
(clap hands on "snap" and "crackle" and "pop")

Ten little chicks go hop, hop, hop.
(hold up ten fingers; open and close hands three times)

Mother, mother, mother hen,
(tuck arms and flap wings)

Sitting on those chicks, all ten.
(cover fist with hand; hold up ten fingers)

"Cheep, cheep, cheep!"
(wiggle fingers)

Who's Hiding My Egg?

A hen lays one egg a day until there are 10 to 12 eggs in the nest. A farmer "tricks" a hen into laying more eggs by taking eggs out of the nest. The hen keeps laying eggs trying to fill the nest!

The setup: Choose one person to be the Hen. The Hen is the Guesser and stands with his back to the group. Everyone else sits in a circle. One person in the circle is quietly chosen to be the Farmer, or the Hider. The Farmer hides the Hen's egg (a toy or pretend egg) under his legs.

The game: The Hen joins the group and tries to guess who's hiding the egg. See who can find the egg using the fewest guesses. Repeat the game with a new Hen (Guesser) and a new Farmer (Hider).

Strategies:

Guesser/Hen: Look at each person for clues. Is someone staring at her legs? Sitting in an unusual position? Or is there someone who is particularly giggly? Maybe he is the egg stealer!

Hider/Farmer: Sit still. Look at the person who is the Hen, not at the place you have hidden the egg!

Hmmmm...

Let's Create

Sitting Hen

WHAT YOU NEED

- ❂ 4 paper plates
- ❂ Stapler
- ❂ White tissue paper, cut in strips 2¹/₂ inches (6 cm) wide
- ❂ Child-safety scissors
- ❂ Glue
- ❂ Red and yellow construction paper
- ❂ Black marker

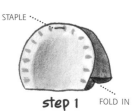

STAPLE

step 1   FOLD IN

step 2

step 3

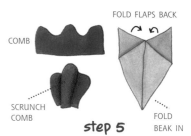

FOLD FLAPS BACK

COMB

SCRUNCH COMB

step 5   FOLD BEAK IN

NATURE NOTES

Egg-citing surprises

A mother hen sits on the eggs for about three weeks before the eggs hatch. The baby chick has to peck its own way through the eggshell. Pretend that you are a baby chick by wrapping your arms tightly around yourself (as if you are giving yourself a hug). Now, slowly, loosen your arms, open them up wide, and stretch in all directions. Peck, peck, peck your way out of the eggshell.

WHAT YOU DO

1. To create the hen's body, place two paper plates together so that the plates' top surfaces face each other. Staple the plates together, at the top edge. Fold the bottom edge of each plate inward. Presto! The hen's body stands upright.

2. To make feathers, fold each tissue-paper strip back and forth (as an accordion fold) several times (the wider the folds, the larger the feathers). Cut the folded tissue into a feather-shape. Glue the feathers to the hen's body.

3. Cut the third paper plate in half to create the hen's wings. Cut fringe along the curved sides. Staple each wing to the hen's body.

4. Cut the center section out of the last plate for the hen's head. Cut the eyes and wattle from red construction paper and glue them onto the head. Use a marker to draw eyeballs.

5. Cut the comb from red construction paper. Scrunch the comb and staple it to the back of the hen's head. Cut the beak from yellow construction paper; fold as shown and glue on. Staple the hen's head to the body.

Toddler Tips: Younger children can paint glue onto the hen's body with a paintbrush, then add the feathers. Draw the eyes, wattle, and beak with markers.

Let's Draw

See the simple shapes in a hen?

Draw the hen's face, making a beak, a wattle, and a comb. You can also draw feathers. Once you get comfortable drawing the hen, try drawing a nest for her to sit in. For a standing hen, draw a full circle for her body and add legs. Have fun! Save some of your favorite hens for the FARM MURAL on pages 124–125.

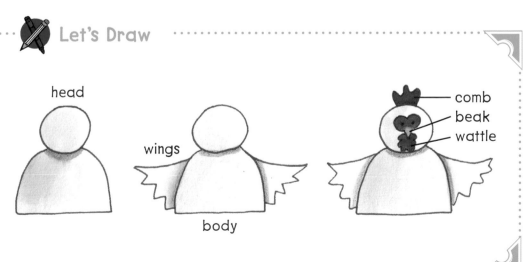

head

wings

body

comb
beak
wattle

Horse Play

Many farm animals are valued because they provide food such as milk, eggs, or meat. The horse is a special farm animal because it can do work to help the farmer. A horse is very strong and can pull or carry heavy loads. It also can run fast and travel long distances!

Let's Create

Giddyup Horse

WHAT YOU NEED

- ☉ Child-safety scissors
- ☉ Brown construction paper
- ☉ Stapler
- ☉ Brown paper lunch bag
- ☉ Newspaper
- ☉ Tape
- ☉ Yarn
- ☉ Markers
- ☉ Package tape or masking tape
- ☉ Cardboard wrapping-paper tube

Giddyup!

step 1

step 2

step 3

What you do

1. Cut the horse's ears from construction paper. Staple the ears to the bottom flap of the paper bag.

2. Crumple newspaper and stuff it into the paper bag. Fold the open end of the bag into a mouth-shape and tape it shut. Use markers to add horse details. Staple on a yarn rein.

3. Use sturdy tape to attach the horse head to the cardboard tube. Giddyup!

More fun: *Add a tail!*

1. Wrap some yarn around your hand and elbow as shown. (The more times you wrap the yarn, the thicker the tail will be.)

2. Tie one end; cut the other end.

3. Thread yarn or elastic through the tail and tie it around your waist.

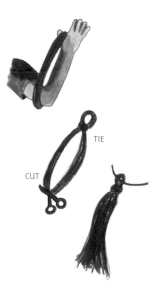

TIE

CUT

Let's Draw

See the simple shapes in a horse?

Draw eyes, a nose, and a mouth. Add a tail.

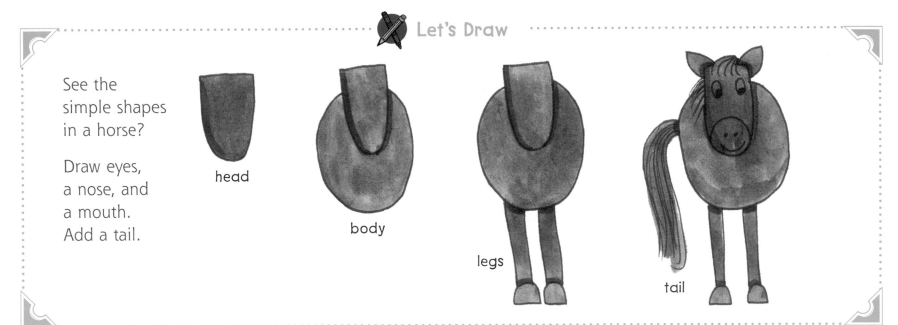

head

body

legs

tail

When working on the farm, horses have to be fast and able to move quickly. Riders have made up games to practice these skills with their horses. Sometimes they compete with other horses in *rodeos*. "Saddle up" and try your skills in the barrel race!

Barrel Races

Create an obstacle course using cones, baskets, or wastepaper containers. Take turns racing "giddyup-style" using the GIDDYUP HORSE (pages 104–105) to go through the obstacle course and back to "start." Use a timer to see how fast you can go.

Let's Sing
Clippity-Clop
(Chant)

Clippity, clippity, clippity-clop,
(alternately slap hands on lap)

This is the way the horses trot.

Clippity, clippity, clippity-clop,

Faster, faster, faster,
(slap hands faster and faster)

Until you …
(slap hands even faster)

Drop!
(slap both hands on the ground)

Toddler Clippity-Clop Ride: Sit on a grown-up's lap. As you chant together, have the grown-up lean you side to side (line 1), gently bounce you up and down (line 2), lean you side to side (line 3), bounce you up and down faster (line 4), raise knees up high (line 5), and finally gently drop you between the knees (line 6)!

LITTLE HANDS
Story Corner™

The Horse in Harry's Room by Syd Hoff

My Pony by Susan Jeffers

A Pony to Love by Christine Taylor-Butler

Moo-o-o-o Who?

Cows are raised on farms for the meat and the milk that they provide.
Do you like hamburgers, milk, cheese, butter, or ice cream?
Well, then—thank a cow!

 **Let's Sing**

Ten Little Cows in the Barn

(Tune: "Ten Little Indians," or chant)

One little, two little, three little cows,
(hold up fingers as you sing)

Four little, five little, six little cows,
Seven little, eight little, nine little cows,
Ten little cows in the barn.
"Moo-o-o-o-oooo!"
(hold fingers at head for horns)

Sing more verses using the names, sounds, and actions of different farm animals.

Let's Draw

See the simple shapes in a cow?

head

body

legs

tail

Try drawing a whole group, or *herd*, of cows. Make a big bull with big horns, a mother cow, and a baby calf.

Colorful Cow Puppet

A boy cow is called a *bull*.
A bull is much larger than a
girl cow and has bigger horns.
Bulls don't produce milk;
only mother cows are milkers.
A baby cow is called a *calf*.
What kind of a cow are you
going to make? Color your
cow any way you like!

Front

step 2

Back

WHAT YOU NEED

- Child-safety scissors
- White, brown, and black construction paper
- White paper lunch bag, or brown
- Glue stick or glue
- Markers
- Watercolors (optional)

WHAT YOU DO

1. Cut a rectangle from white construction paper that's the same size as the bottom flap of the paper bag. Cut the ears from white paper, the horns from the brown paper, and a nose from the black paper.

2. Glue the ears and horns onto the back of the white rectangle. Glue the nose onto the rectangle's front. Glue the rectangle to the bottom flap of the paper bag, covering up any printing.

3. Fold the ears down. Use markers to add eyes. Decorate the cow with markers or watercolors.

Time Saver: If you find white lunch bags without printing on the bottom, just make your cow's face directly on the bag. Glue the horns to the bag's back and the ears just behind the bottom flap. A brown lunch bag can make a brown cow!

 Let's Play

The Cat & the Mouse

On a farm you're likely to find more than just cows in the barn. Mice like to make themselves right at home. Farmers rely on the help of barn cats to rid the barn of mice, but it's not so easy!

Sit in a circle. Choose one person to be the Mouse. The Mouse walks on the outside of the circle, touching each person gently on the head and saying Mouse as he walks by. Eventually he touches someone and says Cat. The Cat stands up quickly and chases the Mouse around the circle. Once both the Cat and the Mouse return to the place where the Cat was sitting, both sit down. Repeat the game until everyone has had a chance to chase and/or be chased.

Baa-a-a, Baa-a-a Sheep

A female (girl) sheep is called a *ewe* (pronounced YEW, or YOU). A male (boy) sheep is called a *ram*. And you already know what a baby sheep is called — a lamb, of course! When a lamb *bleats*, or cries, it sounds just as if it were saying "Baaa!"

Sheep are covered in thick woolly hair called *fleece*. Farmers cut, or *shear*, the fleece, and then the fleece is spun into yarn to make coats, sweaters, hats, mittens, and other clothes.

Imagine being a sheep and wearing a heavy coat of wool. It might be fine in the winter, but in the summertime, you would be very glad to get a haircut, don't you think?

 Let's Play

Mary Says

The setup: Choose someone to be Mary. Everyone else will be Sheep.

The game: Mary tells all the Sheep what to do, similar to the way Simon Says is played. For example, Mary might say "Trot like a horse," "Oink like a pig," or "Strut like a rooster."

If Mary says "Mary Says" *before* the direction, all the Sheep should do what she says. If Mary gives the direction *without* first saying "Mary Says," the Sheep should not follow. Sheep who follow incorrectly are out.

Repeat the game with a new Mary for the next round.

Strategies:

Mary: Talk clearly so that everyone can hear you, but speak quickly. Try to trick the sheep by giving them an instruction like "Mary says touch your nose." Then, instead of you touching your nose, you could touch your ear.

Sheep: Use your ears more than your eyes. Listen carefully!

 Let's Sing

Mary Had a Little Lamb
(Traditional tune, or chant)

Mary had a little lamb,
(hold hands and walk into circle)

Little lamb, little lamb.
(walk out of the circle)

Mary had a little lamb,
(walk into circle)

Its fleece was white as snow.
(walk out of circle)

The lamb liked to run and play,
(hold hands and run in and out of big circle)

Run and play, run and play.
The lamb liked to run and play,
Its fleece was white as snow.

(Repeat the first verse.)

Additional Verses: (1) Eat the grass *(bend down and touch the ground, then stand up)*; (2) Jump up high; (3) Twist and twist.

 Let's Draw

See the simple shapes in a sheep?

head

fleece

legs

Hint: To draw fluffy fleece, start with a circle and then add curvy lines on the outside of the circle. Erase the circle.

On the Farm **111**

 Let's Create

Soft Sheep

WHAT YOU NEED

- Pencil
- White paper (or photocopy)
- Child-safety scissors
- Fine-tipped marker
- Black construction paper
- Hole punch
- Small, white paper plate
- Yarn
- Glue
- Large, white cotton balls

WHAT YOU DO

1. Draw your own sheep's head (page 111), or using a pencil and tracing paper (or a photocopier), copy the SHEEP'S HEAD template. Cut out the copied pattern.

2. Use the marker to make the eyes, nose, and mouth. Cut the sheep's feet from black construction paper.

3. Use a hole punch to make a hole in the top of the paper plate. Loop a piece of yarn through the hole for a hanger.

4. Squeeze glue onto the paper plate. Add cotton balls. Glue on the feet and the head.

SHEEP'S HEAD TEMPLATE

Trace or photocopy the SHEEP'S HEAD template onto a piece of paper. *(Please do not cut this template out of this book. Thank you.)*

LITTLE HANDS
Story Corner™

Sheep in a Jeep by Nancy Shaw

Baa Baa Black Sheep by Iza Trapani

Russell the Sheep by Rob Scotton

Calling All Kids!

Girl goats are called *nanny goats*. Boy goats are called *billy goats*. And baby goats are called *kids*, just like you!

Let's Sing

Billy Goat, Billy Goat

(Tune: "Baa, Baa, Black Sheep," or chant)

Billy goat, billy goat,
(make horns with fingers)

As hungry as can be.
(rub tummy)

Eats and eats,
(open and close hand as if eating)

Everything he sees.
(tickle tummy)

You can eat the grass.
(open and close hand down low)

You can eat the leaves.
(open and close hand up high)

Just make sure,
(wag finger back and forth)

You don't eat me!
(point to self)

(Repeat first verse.)

 Let's Play

Billy Goat Game

The setup: Two people pretend to be hungry Billy Goats. They join hands and raise them up high to form a bridge. All other players form a single line to pass under the bridge.

The game: Sing or chant the first two verses of "BILLY GOAT, BILLY GOAT" (page 114), as the line circles under the bridge. On the last line of the second verse ("You don't eat me!") the Billy Goats lower their arms and capture someone inside. That person then trades places with one of the Billy Goats and the game continues until everyone has had a turn being a Billy Goat.

Strategies:

Billy Goat: Vary the pace of the song to trick the other players. Sing slowly if the person you are trying to catch is far away. Speed up the song if the person you are trying to catch is getting close.

Player: Walk fast when the end of the song is approaching.

LITTLE HANDS Story Corner™

A Girl, a Goat, and a Goose by David McPhail

Gregory, the Terrible Eater by Mitchell Sharmat

The Three Billy-Goats Gruff retold by Ellen Appleby

✋ Let's Create

Bearded Billy Goat

You can tell a billy goat from a nanny goat by its beard or *goatee*. Only boy (male) goats grow beards.

WHAT YOU NEED

- ☻ 2 paper plates
- ☻ Black marker
- ☻ Pencil
- ☻ Crayons
- ☻ Stapler
- ☻ Child-safety scissors

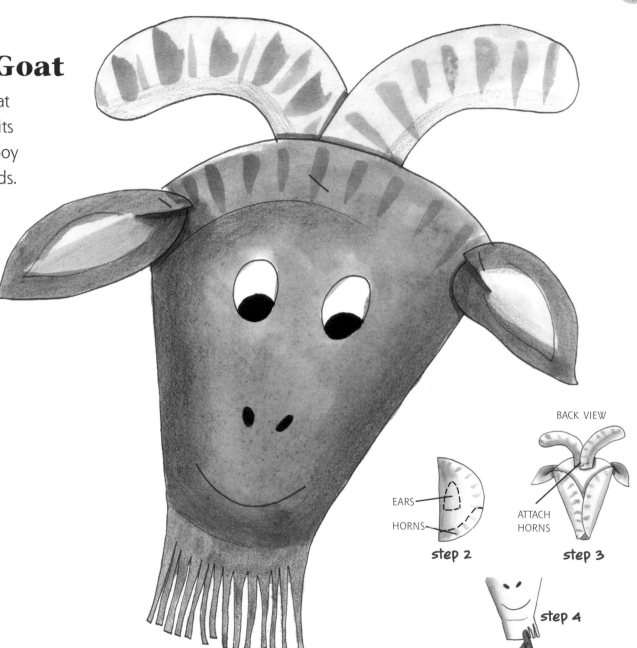

EARS

HORNS

step 2

BACK VIEW

ATTACH HORNS

step 3

step 4

WHAT YOU DO

1. Fold the sides of one paper plate back to create the goat's head. Use a black marker to draw eyes, a nose, and a mouth.

2. Fold the second paper plate in half. Draw the ears and horns as shown. Cut them out, through both thicknesses of the folded paper plate.

3. Color the goat's face and both sides of the ears with crayons. Scrunch the base of the ears and staple to the front of the goat's head. Staple the horns in place. Overlap the plate rims on the back side of the goat and staple together to make a handle.

4. Cut fringe for the goat's beard.

5. Hold the back of the goat as a puppet while singing "BILLY GOAT, BILLY GOAT" (page 114).

Let's Draw

See the simple shapes in a goat?

Try drawing goats that are different sizes.
Can you draw a billy goat, a nanny goat, and a kid?
Have fun! Save some of your favorite goats for
the FARM MURAL on pages 124–125.

Gobble, Gobble, Gobble!

The turkey is a symbol of Thanksgiving Day, as celebrated on the last Thursday in November in the United States. Many families celebrate the holiday by gathering together to give thanks for food, warm homes, and families — and to eat turkey! Today, most of the turkeys we eat are raised on turkey farms. In many regions of the country, you can see groups of wild turkeys strutting their stuff across farm fields, and sometimes even across backyards!

 Let's Sing

Three Little Turkeys Went Out to Play

(Tune: "Three Little Ducks Went Out to Play," or chant)

Three little turkeys went out to play,
(hold up three fingers)

On a bright and sunny day.
(circle arms above head)

When the mama turkey called,
(touch thumb to fingers)

With a gobble, gobble, gobble,
(open and close as if gobbling)

Two little turkeys came,
(bring two fingers from behind back)

Waddle, waddle, waddle.
(tuck arms, lift wings alternately in rhythm)

Repeat stanza at left with two little turkeys and then one little turkey. For the fourth stanza (No little turkeys), use the verses below:

No little turkeys went out to play,
(hold hands out, palms up)

On a bright and sunny day.
(circle arms above head)

When the mama turkey called,
(touch thumb to fingers)

With a gobble, gobble, gobble,
(open and close hand as you gobble really loud)

Three little turkeys came,
(bring three fingers from behind back)

Waddle, waddle, waddle.
(tuck arms, lift wings alternately in rhythm)

Let's Play

Turkey Hide and Seek

Choose someone to be the Farmer. The Farmer closes her eyes and counts to 10 while everyone else hides. When the Farmer opens her eyes, she looks for all the Turkeys. The last Turkey found gets to be the next Farmer.

Strategies:

If a few Turkeys can't be found, the well-hidden Turkeys can make "gobble gobble" sounds to help the Farmer find them.

Gobble, gobble!

NATURE NOTES

Uh-oh! That's an angry turkey!

Wild turkeys have dark feathers to help them blend in with their woodland homes. Their featherless head and the *wattle* that hangs from their neck can change color from gray to bright shades of red, white, and blue. What causes that change? Well, that's how the turkey shows when it is excited or distressed. How do you show excitement or anger? Does your face become slightly *flushed*, or red?

LITTLE HANDS Story Corner™

'Twas the Night Before Thanksgiving by Dav Pilkey

Little Hands Fingerplays & Action Songs by Emily Stetson and Vicky Congdon

Let's Draw

See the simple shapes in a turkey?

Give your turkey legs. Experiment by adding different kinds of feathers. Try drawing round feathers, pointed feathers, short feathers, or tall feathers. Have fun! Save some of your favorite turkeys for the FARM MURAL on pages 124–125.

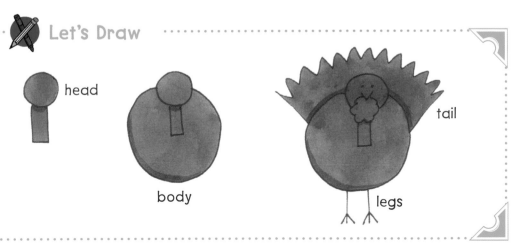

head

body

legs

tail

Turkey Finger Puppet

WHAT YOU NEED

- 2 small paper plates (1½ per puppet)
- Brown paint, in a jar lid
- Paintbrush or sponge
- Child-safety scissors
- Brown, orange, and red construction paper
- Glue
- Marker
- Stapler
- Colorful feathers

WHAT YOU DO

1. Cut one paper plate in half. Paint one half brown. Let dry.

2. Cut the turkey head (brown), beak (orange), and wattle (red) from construction paper. Glue the beak and wattle onto the head. Use a marker to draw eyes.

3. Staple the painted half-plate to the second paper plate with the plates' top surfaces facing in.

4. Glue feathers along the top edge of the back plate. Glue the head to the painted half-plate.

5. Ask a grown-up to help you cut two finger holes through both plates. Stick your fingers through the holes for the turkey's legs.

step 3

step 4

Here Piggy, Piggy

Pigs have very poor eyesight, but fortunately they have good hearing and a great sense of smell. With its big snout, a pig can smell food that is buried underground and then dig it up. Hmmm. Do you think your nose would be good for digging?

A pig will eat almost anything. Some pigs are fed on a mixture of table scraps called pig slop. Imagine your favorite foods, then imagine them all mixed together. Yuck!

 Let's Sing

Piggilty, Piggilty, Pop

(Tune: "Hickory, Dickory Dock," or chant)

Piggilty, piggilty, pop,
(push your nose up with your finger)

The pig eats the pig slop.
(open and close your hand)

He eats,
(make a small circle with your arms out front)

And eats.
(make circle bigger with each "eats")

And eats,
Some more.
Piggilty,
(make circle so big that hands can't touch)

Piggilty,
(make circle even bigger)

POP!
(clap hands loudly)

LITTLE HANDS Story Corner™

Piggies
by Audrey and Don Wood

If You Give a Pig a Pancake
by Laura Numeroff

Olivia by Ian Falconer

Let's Create
Porky Pig Hand Puppet

WHAT YOU NEED

- Child-safety scissors
- Pink construction paper
- Stapler
- 2 paper plates
- Glue stick or glue
- Pink paint, in a jar lid
- Paintbrush or sponge
- Black marker
- Pipe cleaner (4-inch [10 cm] piece per puppet)
- Pencil
- Tape

WHAT YOU DO

1. Paint both paper plates pink; let dry. Cut pig ears, nose, and feet from pink construction paper.

2. Staple the ears and feet to one paper plate. Glue on the nose. Use a black marker to draw eyes and nostrils.

3. Wrap the pipe cleaner around a pencil to make a curly pig's tail.

4. Use a pencil to poke a hole in the back of the second paper plate. Stick the uncurled end of the tail into the hole and tape it to the inside of the plate to hold it in place.

5. Staple the front and back of the pig together. Leave the bottom open to fit your hand.

step 1

step 3

OUT

INSIDE

step 4

 Let's Play

Farm Chores Obstacle Course

A farmer has so much to do,
He works and works the whole day through!

Farmers work very hard. Many chores, such as milking the cows and collecting eggs from the hens, must be done every day. And all of the animals must be fed and given plenty of clean water to drink.

Pretend you are a farmer, feeding the pigs and other animals, in these fun games!

The setup: Make the obstacle course by setting up all of the games as described below.

Feed the pigs: Fill one bucket with balls (pigs' "food"). Place an empty bucket (food trough) 15 to 20 feet (5 to 7 m) away.

Herd the sheep: Line up four buckets about 5 feet (2 m) apart.

Lasso a cow: Set two soft drink bottles (the pretend cows) 4 feet (1.5 m) apart. Make a hoop from foil or the rim of a paper plate.

Collect eggs: Fill a "hen's nest" bucket with toy or pretend eggs. Place an empty bucket for collecting the eggs 20 feet (7 m) away.

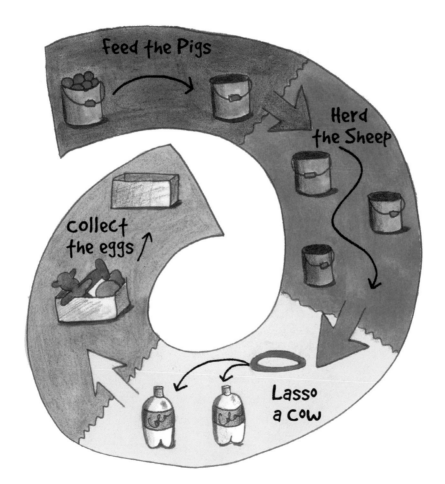

Feed the Pigs

Herd the Sheep

collect the eggs

Lasso a cow

The game: Players form a line behind the first obstacle. When the first person gets halfway through the course, the next person in line can begin. See how quickly you can get all your chores done!

Variation: Play in two teams for more of a challenge!

Feed the pigs: Take a piece of food (ball) and run over to place it into the pig's food trough.

Herd the sheep: Herd the sheep as you race around the buckets on your pretend horse.

Lasso a cow: Take a "lasso" (the hoop) and toss it around a "cow" (a soda bottle).

Collect eggs: Grab an "egg" from the "hen's nest" and run to drop it into the collecting basket.

 Let's Create

Farm Mural

A mural is a large picture that you make and hang on a wall. You can use all of the farm animal pictures that you drew throughout this chapter to create a farm mural.

You can create an individual mural on a brown grocery bag or a group mural on a long piece of butcher paper. And, aside from painting on the paper, you can paste on pictures that you drew or cut out, you can paste on three-dimensional art that sticks out from the paper, and you can add just about anything that you can think of including leaves, real shells, and beads.

WHAT YOU NEED

- Child-safety scissors
- Paper grocery bag
- Paint, in a jar lid
- Plastic fork
- Craft or Popsicle sticks
- Glue stick and/or glue
- Animal pictures (drawn, or cut out from old magazines)
- Sponges, brushes & assorted objects to apply paint
- Cotton balls

WHAT YOU DO

1. Cut a grocery bag along the seam. Cut off the bottom flap of the bag.

2. Open the bag flat, with the unprinted side facing up.

3. Create grass by dipping a plastic fork in paint and pressing it all along the bottom of the paper.

4. Create a barn by gluing craft or Popsicle sticks onto the paper in a barn shape.

5. Draw or cut out pictures of farm animals. Use a glue stick to glue them to your picture.

6. Paint the background to your farm mural. Use a variety of things to apply the paint: sponges, cotton balls, bottle caps, and bubble wrap.

7. Create clouds by gluing cotton balls to the mural. How many animals are on your FARM MURAL?

Index

More Good Books from Williamson

Welcome to Williamson Books! Our books are available from your bookseller or directly from Williamson Books at Ideals Publications. Please see the next page for ordering information or to visit our website. Thank you.

All books are suitable for children ages 3 through 7, and are 120 to 128 pages, softcover, 10 x 8, $12.95, unless otherwise noted.

· · · · · · · · · · · · · · · · · · · ·

Parents' Choice Approved
Fingerplays & Action Songs
Seasonal Activities & Creative Play for 2- to 6-Year-Olds
by Emily Stetson & Vicky Congdon

Parents' Choice Gold Award
Fun with My 5 Senses
Activities to Build Learning Readiness
by Sarah A. Williamson

Parents' Choice Recommended
At the Zoo!
Explore the Animal World with Craft Fun
by Judy Press

Parents' Choice Recommended
Easy Art Fun!
Do-It-Yourself Crafts for Beginning Readers
(A *Little Hands*® Read-&-Do book)
by Jill Frankel Hauser

Parents' Choice Approved
Little Hands Create!
Art & Activities for Kids Ages 3 to 6
by Mary Dall

ForeWord Magazine Children's Book of the Year Finalist
All Around Town
Exploring Your Community Through Craft Fun
by Judy Press

Creating Clever Castles & Cars (from Boxes & Other Stuff)
by Mari Mitchell

Parent's Guide Children's Media Award
Alphabet Art
With A to Z Animal Art & Fingerplays
by Judy Press

Parents' Choice Recommended
Early Learning Skill-Builders
Colors, Shapes, Numbers & Letters
by Mary Tomczyk

Parents' Choice Approved
Paper Plate Crafts
Creative Art Fun for 3- to 7-year-olds
by Laura Check

Kindergarten Success
Helping children excel right from the start
by Jill Frankel Hauser

Parent's Guide Classic Award
Real Life Award
The Little Hands ART BOOK
Exploring Arts & Crafts with 2- to 6-Year-Olds
by Judy Press

Little Hands® Celebrate America!
Learning about the U.S. through Crafts & Activities
by Jill Frankel Hauser